Taxcafe.co.uk Tax Guides

How to Avoid Inheritance Tax

By Carl Bayley BSc ACA

Important Legal Notices:

TAXCafe™
TAX GUIDE – "How to Avoid Inheritance Tax"

Published by:
Taxcafe UK Limited
214 High Street
Kirkcaldy
Tel: (01592) 560081
Email address: team@taxcafe.co.uk

First Edition   May 2003
Second Edition   April 2004
Third Edition   April 2005
Fourth Edition   June 2006

ISBN 1 904608 45 0

About the Author

Carl Bayley is the author of a number of tax guides designed specifically for the layman. Carl's particular speciality is his ability to take the weird, complex and inexplicable world of taxation and to set it out in the kind of clear, straightforward language that taxpayers themselves can understand. As he often says himself, "my job is to translate 'tax' into English".

Carl takes the same approach when speaking on taxation, a role he has undertaken with some relish on a number of occasions, including his highly acclaimed series of seminars at the London Homebuyer Show and his annual 'Budget Breakfast' for the Institute of Chartered Accountants in England & Wales.

In addition to being a recognised author and speaker on the subject, Carl has also spoken on property taxation on BBC radio and television. Most recently, he has also appeared on Irish television too.

A Chartered Accountant by training, Carl began his professional life in 1983, in the Birmingham office of one of the 'Big 4' accountancy firms. He qualified as a double prize-winner and immediately began specialising in taxation.

After 17 years honing his skills with major firms, Carl began the new millennium in January 2000 by launching his own Edinburgh-based tax consultancy practice. The rapid growth of this practice led, in late 2005, to the formation of Bayley Miller Limited, through which Carl now provides advice on a wide variety of UK taxation issues, especially property taxation, Inheritance Tax planning and matters affecting small and medium-sized businesses.

Carl has recently completed three years as Chairman of the Institute Members in Scotland group (2003-2006) and is also a former member of the governing Council of the Institute of Chartered Accountants in England and Wales (2003-2005).

When he isn't working, Carl takes on the equally taxing challenges of hill walking and writing poetry. Carl lives in Edinburgh with his partner Isabel and has four children.

Dedications and Thanks

For the Past,

Given the subject matter of this book, it seems appropriate to dedicate it to the memory of those I have loved and lost:

To my beloved friend and companion, Dawson, who waited so patiently for me to come home every night and who left me in the middle of our last walk together;

To my dear grandparents, Arthur, Doris and Winifred;

And, most of all, to my beloved mother, Diana, who made it all possible.

They left me with nothing I could spend, but everything I need.

For the Present,

As usual, I would also like to dedicate this book to Isabel, my 'life support system', whose unflinching support has seen me through the best and the worst. Whether anyone will ever call me a 'great man' I do not know, but I do know that I have a great woman behind me.

Without her help, support and encouragement, this book, and the others I have written, could never have been.

For the Future,

Finally, I would also like to dedicate this book to four young people who have provided me with a continuing personal interest in this subject: Michelle, Louise, James and Robert.

I can only hope that I, in turn, will also be able to leave them with everything that they need.

Thanks

Sincere thanks are due to my good friend, colleague and 'comrade-in-arms', Nick, who believed in me long before I did.

Thanks also to the rest of the Taxcafe team for their help in making these books far more successful than I could ever have dreamed.

And thanks to Ann for keeping us right!

C.B., Edinburgh, June 2006

Contents

Contents Cont...

Contents Cont...

Contents Cont...

Contents Cont...

Contents Cont...

Chapter 1

Introduction

1.1   THERE ARE TWO CERTAINTIES IN LIFE

Generally speaking, I find that the oldest sayings are the truest. One old saying is "There are only two certainties in life: Death and Taxes".

The place where these two great 'certainties' meet is 'Inheritance Tax', and it is through the medium of this tax that Revenue & Customs will aim to get their final pound of flesh from you, just as you have departed this life.

Most people spend their lifetime trying to accumulate a reasonable amount of wealth, to take care of themselves in their old age and then to pass on any remaining surplus to their children. Much of the Government's fiscal policy is aimed at encouraging this type of behaviour.

It is somewhat unfair then, that without careful planning and a great deal of pre-emptive action, most families will ultimately face a huge Inheritance Tax bill.

Unchecked, this tax bill will rob your family of a significant proportion of their rightful inheritance – up to 40% of it, in fact.

Most people are absolutely appalled at this prospect which, of course, is where Inheritance Tax planning comes in!

Some years ago, the Labour Party accused the then Conservative Government of allowing Inheritance Tax to become a 'voluntary tax', paid only by the unwary, ill-advised and unprepared taxpayer, whilst wealthier taxpayers took good (but expensive) professional advice and avoided the tax.

Certainly, there was an element of truth in this accusation. Furthermore, it remained almost equally true for the best part of another seven years since, despite fears to the contrary, 'New Labour' initially did little to change the Inheritance Tax regime after sweeping into power in 1997.

However, on 10th December 2003, it became quite clear that the 'phoney war' was over, as Chancellor of the Exchequer, Gordon Brown, announced plans for a new Income Tax benefit-in-kind charge targeted at those families attempting to plan for the inevitable.

That charge, the 'Pre-Owned Assets Charge', is surely one of the worst examples we have ever seen of the Government's well known tendency to 'use a sledgehammer to crack a nut' and it came into force on 6th April 2005. Very soon now, on 31st January 2007, we will see the first actual payments of tax arising as a result.

Not satisfied with getting this rather draconian measure onto the statute books, Gordon Brown turned up the heat even further on 22nd March 2006, with a savage attack on trusts which I have heard one expert describe as "the most fundamental change to the trust taxation regime in over 20 years."

Nevertheless, despite these recent dramatic changes to the Inheritance Tax planning environment, what remains true to this day is the fact that it is the moderately wealthy members of society who suffer the greatest proportionate burden of Inheritance Tax when compared with their overall wealth.

In my experience, Inheritance Tax tends to be a tax which is predominantly paid by the modestly wealthy citizens of middle England (as well as middle Scotland, Wales and Northern Ireland too).

The problem for many people in the middle wealth bracket is that they face a fundamental dichotomy.

On the one hand they have, on paper, sufficient wealth to leave their family with a very substantial tax burden when they pass away.

On the other hand, however, they do not really have a great deal of disposable income, despite leading reasonably modest lifestyles.

This means that the very simple expedient of simply giving all of their surplus wealth away is, in practical terms, simply not an option.

Recent trends have added to this problem. The rapid increase in property values over the last decade has pushed more and more people into the Inheritance Tax bracket, especially in the 'hotspots' like London and the South East and other desirable areas, such as my home town, Edinburgh.

The second factor adding impetus to the 'asset rich/cash poor' situation, which many people now find themselves in, is the current still relatively low level of return on investments.

In short, what this means is that a lot of capital produces only a modest income, leaving a great many people with very little real wealth today but serious Inheritance Tax problems for tomorrow!

In my working life I see the stress, worry and anxiety which this situation creates on a regular basis. I am firmly of the opinion that the emotional strain which Inheritance Tax places on so many people is so detrimental that it far outweighs any benefits which the Government may derive from collecting the tax.

Personally, I would dearly love to see this immoral and evil tax abolished as soon as possible.

In the meantime, however, I am afraid to say that we seem to be stuck with Inheritance Tax for the foreseeable future as sadly, its abolition did not appear in any major party's General Election manifesto last year.

As ever, there remain two effective ways to avoid Inheritance Tax:

- Die poor, or
- Plan ahead

Most of us find the first option somewhat unpalatable, and also quite difficult to achieve without a remarkable sense of timing!

Until recently, 'planning ahead' has also been seen as the prerogative of the very wealthiest members of society, leaving the moderately wealthy to pick up the bill!

However, my aim in this guide is to help put an end to this situation.

If the Government is still prepared to allow Inheritance Tax to be even partly 'voluntary', albeit to a far lesser extent than previously, then why should <u>anyone</u> volunteer?

Early and careful planning is the key to reducing the eventual Inheritance Tax burden on your family and you don't need to be a millionaire to do it. Or to <u>need</u> to do it either, for that matter!

Besides which, a great many people are surprised to discover that, when they do add up all of their assets, they are, in fact, millionaires anyway. On paper, at least.

Whilst some tax can still be saved through 'last-minute' planning, a great deal more unnecessary tax can be avoided by planning for death and taxes throughout your lifetime. Read on and I will show you how.

1.2   GUIDE OVERVIEW

In this opening chapter, we will start by taking a brief look at some background issues important to an understanding of the rest of the guide.

Following that, in Chapters 2 and 3, we will cover some of the basics – how the tax is calculated, who pays it and which branch of the Government administers it. All of this comes under the general heading of 'know your enemy' because it is important to understand what you're up against before you start to make any plans to combat it.

We then move on, in Chapters 4 to 6 look at what exemptions are available and how to maximise them, both during your lifetime and through your Will.

Chapter 7 covers the important area of business property relief, perhaps the most valuable piece of equipment in our Inheritance Tax avoidance armoury.

After tidying up a few loose ends in Chapter 8, we will then move into the realm of trusts in Chapters 9 and 10 and we will see what powerful tools these vehicles can provide in the battle against Inheritance Tax.

Chapter 11 reminds us that there is a 'bigger picture' than merely avoiding Inheritance Tax and here we will widen our sights to take in other aspects of estate preservation. This is reinforced in Chapter 12 with a look at the interaction between Inheritance Tax and Capital Gains Tax.

In Chapter 13 we move on to the all-important issue of the family home and this will also dominate our review of the pre-owned assets charge in Chapter 14.

Bringing things (almost) to a close, Chapter 15 provides a useful 'whole life and beyond' timetable for effective Inheritance Tax planning which sets everything else we have learned into context and also reassures us that, whilst it's never too early to start planning, it's never too late either!

Lastly, in Chapter 16, we cover perhaps the most drastic of all planning techniques, with a guide to emigration, as well as a look at the advantages available to those who have already done it.

At more than double the size of our previous edition, this guide must surely now have something of value for everyone and provides a useful tool in the battle against the Government's most despicable form of taxation.

1.3   A BRIEF HISTORY OF INHERITANCE TAX

Inheritance Tax, as we know it today, arrived in 1986, the brainchild of Margaret Thatcher and her then Chancellor, Nigel Lawson. 'IHT', as the tax would become known to those of us who were young accountancy students at the time, was little more than a re-branding of its predecessor, Capital Transfer Tax (fondly known as 'CTT').

Capital Transfer Tax, in turn, had replaced the earlier and rather more draconian Estate Duty, which had, in its day, played a major part in turning many of Britain's stately homes into amusement parks!

It is quite ironic that Inheritance Tax should have such a long lineage because it is, of course, one's descendants who will suffer its effects.

The principal difference between Inheritance Tax and its predecessors is the fact that there is a general exemption for most lifetime transfers to other individuals.

This is part of the reason behind the accusations that Inheritance Tax is a voluntary tax, since simply giving all of one's wealth away would initially seem to be an easy way to escape the tax altogether.

However, inevitably, as we will see later in this guide, Inheritance Tax is not quite that easy to avoid. You would have to survive for at least seven years after leaving yourself completely destitute (and homeless), for a start!

1.4   WHY WORRY?

Of course **you** won't actually have to pay any Inheritance Tax on your own estate. Furthermore, for most people, everything can safely be left to their widow, widower or registered civil partner free from any Inheritance Tax.

And, if you have no other dependants or potential beneficiaries to care about, but simply resent paying any unnecessary tax, you can simply leave it all to charity.

But most people **_do_** have someone they care about. Usually they have children or other family or friends whom they want to see benefit from the assets which they have built up in their lifetime and they don't want to see the Government taking 40% of it away.

Even if, in the first instance, you are leaving everything tax free to your surviving spouse or registered civil partner, your accumulated wealth will eventually be hit by Inheritance Tax if you don't plan ahead.

As we will see later in the guide, you need to take action **_now_** in order to safeguard your family's future prosperity.

Alternatively, you may be in the position of being the potential beneficiary yourself, trying to get an elderly relative to plan for the preservation of your inheritance.

Either way, there is plenty to worry about!

But Am I Wealthy Enough to Need to Worry?

Most people are quite surprised to discover just how much they are actually worth. How often have you heard someone say "I'm worth more dead than alive". Very often, especially as we get older, it's true. (In pure financial terms only, of course.)

This is basically because it takes an enormous amount of capital just to support one person. When that person dies, the capital which was previously tied up in supporting them is freed. (After the Government gets its share of it, that is!)

Hence, although you may not feel particularly wealthy, you may still find that you have a large potential Inheritance Tax bill.

You'd be amazed at just how many 'paper millionaires' there are these days. Take a look at this example:

Example

Rosemary, a widow, owns a large detached house, which her late husband left to her. The house is bigger than she really needs, but it was the former marital home, so she is quite attached to it. She has been advised that its current market value is £450,000.

Rosemary is retired and lives off her savings and an investment portfolio which was also left to her by her late husband. Although these produce an income of only £19,500 per annum, their total value is approximately £425,000.

Whilst they were married, Rosemary and her husband enjoyed collecting paintings. She recently had their modest collection valued and was astounded to discover that it is now worth £80,000.

Rosemary also has some jewellery, some silver and a few antiques. Altogether, these are worth £40,000. Lastly, she has a small car, worth £5,000.

Nobody would call Rosemary rich by any stretch of the imagination. She's living off only £19,500 a year. But add it all up and you will find that she is a millionaire!

This means that Rosemary's family has a potential Inheritance Tax bill of £286,000!

And you don't need to be anywhere near as 'wealthy' as Rosemary to have an Inheritance Tax problem. Once your estate is worth over £285,000, you have a potential exposure to tax at 40% on the excess.

£285,000! What's that these days? A flat, a car and a few savings and you're there!

So, yes, generally speaking, if you can afford to buy this guide, you probably are wealthy enough to need to worry about Inheritance Tax!

1.5   WHERE DOES THE TAX COME FROM?

The statistics on the main sources of Inheritance Tax make interesting reading:

- 41% comes from *people's own homes!*

- 26% comes from cash (including savings accounts, deposit accounts, etc.).

- 12% comes from quoted shares and securities.

- The remaining balance comes from household personal effects, insurance proceeds and other land holdings.

The top item on the list is the family home, which proves that this tax is not, as the Government would like to have you think, predominantly raised on the rich.

Inheritance Tax is mainly derived from the estates of normal people whose only 'crime' is simply to have been careful with their finances all their life.

We will return to the subject of Inheritance Tax on the family home later in the guide.

1.6 MARRIED COUPLES & REGISTERED CIVIL PARTNERS

Throughout this guide, you will see me refer many times to 'married couples', 'husbands and wives' or 'spouses', as well as to 'widows' and 'widowers'.

Since 5th December 2005, same-sex couples have been able to enter into a registered civil partnership affording them all of the same legal rights and obligations as a married couple.

This equality of treatment also extends to all UK tax law, including Inheritance Tax, and it is probably in the realm of Inheritance Tax that the Civil Partnership Act has provided the greatest tax saving potential for same-sex couples, putting them, as it does, on a par with heterosexual couples.

Throughout the rest of this guide, any reference to 'married couples', 'husbands and wives' or 'spouses' should be taken to also include registered civil partners.

Equally, when I refer to 'widows' and 'widowers', this will also include the surviving partner in a registered civil partnership whose partner has passed away.

The 'widow's loan scheme' in Section 4.6, for example, will work just as well for registered civil partners as it does for married couples.

It is important to remember however, that unless specified to the contrary, the tax treatment being outlined will be available to legally married couples and same-sex couples in a registered civil partnership only.

Remember also that marriage, and now registered civil partnership, is not always advantageous for tax purposes. It really is a case of 'for better or worse'!

1.7 CHANGES TO THE UK TAX AUTHORITIES

On 18th April 2005, two massive institutions, namely the Inland Revenue and HM Customs and Excise, were merged into one single giant UK tax authority: Her Majesty's Revenue and Customs.

Whilst some readers may be more familiar with the two former tax authorities, all UK taxes are now dealt with by HM Revenue & Customs. In this guide, I will therefore now refer only to Revenue & Customs when describing the tax authorities.

Nevertheless, different departments within the organisation continue to deal with matters which previously concerned the Inland Revenue or Customs & Excise. Hence, it is now the Capital Taxes Office of Revenue & Customs which deals with Inheritance Tax.

1.8 TAX YEARS

Inheritance Tax, like most other UK taxes, is administered by reference to the UK tax year. The UK tax year is the period of twelve months ending on 5th April.

Thus, for example, the 2006/2007 tax year is the year ending 5th April 2007.

Any references to the 'tax year' in this guide must therefore be construed accordingly.

Other periods are, however, also important for Inheritance Tax purposes and a reference to a 'period of seven years' or a 'period of more than three years' in this guide, for example, means a strict period of calendar years rather than tax years.

1.9 TRUST TERMINOLOGY

Trust concepts and terminology are key to an understanding of Inheritance Tax.

As well as the various types of trust, we will encounter important concepts such as 'interest in possession' and 'life interest' throughout this guide.

The meaning of these terms will be explained in Chapter 9.

1.10   A WORD OF CAUTION ABOUT INHERITANCE TAX PLANNING

All tax planning needs to be undertaken carefully and in full knowledge of all of the particular circumstances of the taxpayer's own individual case.

This is probably never more true than in the case of Inheritance Tax planning, where a detailed review of the individual's own situation is vital to success.

At the present time, the full impact of the 'Pre-Owned Asset Regime' and its resultant Income Tax charges (see Chapter 14) is still not yet fully understood. At the time of writing, this new regime has been in force for only just over a year and it is still more than eight months until anyone will actually have to pay any tax on these charges.

On top of this, the statutory provisions required to enforce Gordon Brown's latest attack on the taxation of trusts were still making their way through Parliament at the time of writing this guide.

In this guide, I have therefore been able to provide only a brief examination of these two new regimes, further details of which are still emerging on a regular basis.

The reader must also bear in mind the general nature of this guide. Individual circumstances vary and the tax implications of an individual's actions will vary with them. For this reason, it is always vital to get professional advice before undertaking any tax planning or other transactions which may have tax implications.

The author cannot accept any responsibility for any loss which may arise as a consequence of any action taken, or any decision to refrain from action taken, as a result of reading this guide.

Chapter 2

Inheritance Tax Principles

2.1 TRANSFERS OF VALUE

"Inheritance Tax is payable on death. Everyone knows that, don't they?"

Like so many things which 'everyone knows' (like "man will never fly" and "an iceberg will never sink a ship") this is **WRONG**!

Now, admittedly, the vast majority of the Inheritance Tax which the Government collects arises on the occasion of someone's death, this is true. Furthermore, most of the remainder also arises due to attempts made by taxpayers to offload some of their wealth before then.

However, what actually triggers Inheritance Tax is not death, but any 'transfer of value'.

In principle, Inheritance Tax is chargeable on any 'transfer of value' made by any person at any time. Thankfully, however, there are a number of exemptions which apply and these help to ensure that we don't have to pay Gordon Brown 40% every time we give the kids their pocket money.

We'll look at these various exemptions later, in Chapters 4 and 6.

The reasons why we tend to think of Inheritance Tax as applying mainly on death are really three-fold:

i) On death, we are inevitably forced to transfer our entire wealth to others, thus causing, for most of us, the biggest 'transfer of value' of our lives.
ii) Most lifetime transfers to other individuals are exempt, or at least only become chargeable in the event of death within seven years.
iii) The name of the tax implies (falsely) that it is only related to death.

What is a 'Transfer of Value'?

A transfer of value occurs whenever you dispose of something and, as a result, your total net wealth is reduced. Your 'total net wealth' is referred to as your 'estate' and we will explore this concept further in Section 2.9.

What you are 'disposing of' may be money or may be any other asset with monetary value. Furthermore, it is the reduction in your own net wealth which generates the 'transfer of value', not necessarily the value of the asset disposed of. We will see an example of this a little later.

Any disposal of wealth by way of a 'transaction at arm's length' between unconnected persons is not treated as a 'transfer of value'. Hence, the most basic transactions in life, such as buying the weekly grocery, will not be classed as a 'transfer of value', even though your total net wealth is inevitably reduced.

Furthermore, when dealing at arm's length with unconnected persons, merely striking a 'poor bargain' will not be a transfer of value.

Example

John buys a car for £5,000 from Alexei, a second-hand car dealer. It turns out, however, that the car is an absolute wreck, worth at best around £800!

Poor John. However, at least there is no 'transfer of value' here, since John and Alexei are not connected.

If, on the other hand, John had bought the car from his sister, Janet, there would have been a transfer of value, as they are 'connected persons' (see Appendix C).

Nevertheless, a transaction with a connected person will not give rise to any transfer of value, as long as it is carried out in the same way as it would have been if it had been an arm's length transaction with an unconnected person.

Example

Mick wants to buy his father's house. His father, Keith, obtains an independent valuation on the house, which indicates that it is worth £200,000. He therefore sells the house to Mick for this amount.

Unbeknown to Mick, Keith and the independent valuer, plans for a new bypass are just about to be announced, as a result of which the house's value will increase dramatically.

This may look like a 'transfer of value' but it isn't because Mick and Keith have struck the same bargain as would have been struck between unconnected persons.

The Amount of the 'Transfer of Value'

As stated above, a 'transfer of value' occurs whenever you make a disposal which is not at arm's length and, as a result, there is a reduction in your total net wealth (your estate).

The simplest type of 'transfer of value' is therefore a straightforward gift.

If you give someone £10,000 in cash that is a 'transfer of value' of £10,000, if you give someone a painting worth £5,000, that is a 'transfer of value' of £5,000.

A 'transfer of value' also occurs, however, when sales take place between connected persons at an undervalue or at an overvalue.

If you sell your son a painting for £2,000 when it is, in fact, worth £10,000, that is a 'transfer of value' of £8,000. If you buy a car from your daughter and pay her £5,000, when the car is worth only £1,000, then that is a 'transfer of value' of £4,000.

But what is important to remember is that it is the reduction in the value of your overall estate which gives rise to the 'transfer of value'.

Example

Bjorn has a set of six antique chairs, worth £20,000. He gives his son Benny one of the chairs. The value of this single chair, or any other chair which is not part of a complete set, is only £1,500.

However, the 'transfer of value' here is not the value of Benny's single chair, £1,500.

No, the 'transfer of value' is the reduction in the value of Bjorn's overall estate. Previously, he had a set of chairs worth £20,000. After the gift to Benny, he has five chairs worth £1,500 each, a total of £7,500.

Hence, the reduction in the value of Bjorn's estate, and thus the amount of the 'transfer of value', is £12,500.

2.2   WHO IS LIABLE FOR INHERITANCE TAX?

For UK domiciled individuals, Inheritance Tax arises on:

- The net value of their entire estate (see Section 2.9) at the time of their death, wherever situated,

  Less:

  i)   The 'nil rate band' (£285,000 for deaths occurring during the year ending 5th April 2007).
  ii)   Any other applicable exemptions and reliefs (see Chapter 4).

  AND

- Certain lifetime gifts and other transfers (see Chapter 5).

What Does 'Domiciled' Mean?

Broadly speaking, 'Domicile' is a concept similar to nationality and, for most people, it will be pretty obvious whether or not they are UK domiciled.

Nevertheless, 'Domicile' does not entirely correspond to nationality, and can sometimes be a highly complex matter.

15

We will return to a detailed examination of the concept of Domicile in Chapter 16.

Deemed Domicile

Before those of you born in a sunnier climate start to rejoice, you should note that you will also be deemed to be UK domiciled for Inheritance Tax purposes, and taxed accordingly, if you have been Tax Resident here for at least 17 out of the last 20 UK tax years (years ended 5th April).

Note that this does not affect your position in respect of Income Tax or Capital Gains Tax. For this reason, it remains worth retaining foreign Domicile, even if you have deemed UK Domicile for Inheritance Tax purposes.

Emigration

A person who ceases to be UK domiciled will also continue to have deemed UK domicile for Inheritance Tax purposes for three years after ceasing to be UK domiciled under general principles.

Emigration is covered in more detail in Chapter 16.

Immigrants And Trusts

Those who did not have a UK 'Domicile of Origin' (see Section 16.2), but who have subsequently acquired actual or deemed UK domicile, may generally exclude non-UK assets which were transferred into a trust for their benefit before they acquired UK domicile, or deemed UK domicile, and which are still held therein.

Non-Domiciled Individuals

If you are neither UK Domiciled, nor deemed to be UK Domiciled, as explained above, then Inheritance Tax will generally only arise on any UK assets which you hold, including land and buildings situated within the UK.

Again, this liability arises on death or in the event of certain lifetime transfers, which we will cover later in the guide.

Foreign currency bank accounts held by a non-Domiciled individual at the time of their death are generally exempt from Inheritance Tax, even when held with a UK bank or the Post Office. For the purpose of this exemption, the deceased must also be non-UK resident at the time of death.

A few countries (see Appendix B) have Double Tax Treaties with the UK which may affect your position if you are domiciled there. This will sometimes also apply to the question of 'deemed domicile'.

2.3   WHO ACTUALLY PAYS THE TAX?

Despite my comments in Section 2.1, most Inheritance Tax does, of course, still arise on death and, naturally, the deceased is not around to pick up the bill!

The liability for Inheritance Tax arising on death will generally fall on the deceased's Personal Representatives (who must settle it out of the assets of the estate).

There are, however, some exceptions to this general rule, as follows:

i)   Where specific property vests in a beneficiary (e.g. "I leave my house to my sister Julie").

ii) Where a beneficiary becomes entitled to a life interest in property under the terms of the Will.

iii) Where a bequest is made on the specific condition that the beneficiary meets the Inheritance Tax arising out of their legacy.

iv) Where property is already held in trust (as explained in Chapter 9).

In cases under (i), (ii) and (iii) above, it is the beneficiaries themselves who must bear the tax.

However, where specific bequests are being made (as in (i) above), it is possible to draw up your Will in such a way that the Inheritance Tax falls on your Personal Representatives (to be settled out of the general assets of your estate).

For property already held in trust, as in (iv) above, the Inheritance Tax may fall on the trustees or on a beneficiary of that trust, depending on the exact circumstances.

2.4   GROSSING UP

The amount of Inheritance Tax payable on a specific asset or bequest may be affected by whether or not it is paid by the Personal Representatives.

This is due to the procedure known as 'Grossing Up' and is best explained by way of a short example.

Example

John leaves his eldest son Paul a house worth £90,000, on condition that he settles any tax arising. He also leaves his younger son George the sum of £90,000 in cash, stating in his Will that this sum should be free of all taxes and other encumbrances.

As Paul has to settle the Inheritance Tax on his bequest directly, he will pay Inheritance Tax at a straightforward rate of 40%, i.e. £36,000.

The Inheritance Tax on George's bequest will, however, be paid by John's Personal Representatives, Ringo & Co. This brings into play the procedure known as 'Grossing Up'.

In other words, George's bequest must be grossed up to account for the Inheritance Tax being paid out of John's estate.

The 'Grossing Up' factor is 2/3rds. Hence, an additional two thirds must be added to George's bequest of £90,000, producing a grossed up amount of £150,000 (£90,000 PLUS two thirds of £90,000, i.e. £60,000).

The Inheritance Tax due on this bequest is therefore £60,000 (i.e. £150,000 x 40%).

*As can readily be seen, this is equal to the amount of the 'Grossing Up',
meaning that Ringo & Co. can now give the original sum of £90,000 to
George free of any further tax liabilities.*

NOTE: In this example, for the sake of simplicity, I have ignored
the impact of any applicable reliefs and exemptions, including the
nil rate band. I have also assumed that there are sufficient other
assets within the estate to enable the Personal Representatives to
settle the Inheritance Tax liability arising from George's bequest.

'Grossing Up' becomes very important when, as in the Example
above, a number of different beneficiaries are involved.

However, in the simple case of a single beneficiary, it has no effect
since the same total amount of Inheritance Tax will always be
payable out of the estate.

The impact of 'Grossing Up' is simply to decide how much
Inheritance Tax is borne by each beneficiary.

Someone will always be entitled to the residuary amount left in
the estate after dealing with all of the specific bequests and it is
that person who will ultimately suffer the impact of the 'Grossing
Up' calculations.

2.5   WHO ARE THE PERSONAL REPRESENTATIVES?

Where the deceased has left a Will, their executors, as appointed
under the terms of their Will, are their Personal Representatives.

In the case of a person dying intestate (i.e. without a valid Will),
the person applying for a grant of representation (i.e. probate), or
confirmation in Scotland, will be the Personal Representative.

Where no Personal Representative has been appointed by the court
within twelve months after the end of the month of death then
the deceased's beneficiaries will be required to fulfil the obligations
regarding payment of Inheritance Tax, delivery of accounts, etc,
which would normally fall on the Personal Representatives.

2.6 WHO PAYS THE TAX ON LIFETIME TRANSFERS?

The primary responsibility for any Inheritance Tax arising on lifetime transfers falls on the transferor. It is possible, however, to stipulate that the transferee should bear any Inheritance Tax arising (see Memorandum 2 in Appendix D).

Additional Inheritance Tax liabilities frequently arise when the transferor dies within seven years of a lifetime transfer. These liabilities usually fall on the transferee.

'Grossing Up' can also apply to lifetime transfers, although a lower 'grossing up' rate of one quarter applies.

Inheritance Tax on lifetime transfers is examined in more detail in Chapter 5 below.

2.7 COLLECTION OF TAX

As we can see from the preceding sections, the liability for Inheritance Tax may fall on any of:

- The transferor,
- The transferee,
- The deceased's Personal Representatives, or
- The deceased's beneficiaries.

Naturally, Revenue & Customs, will, in the first instance, attempt to collect the tax due from the correct party.

However, if they encounter any difficulty in collecting the tax from the correct party, they will look to any other party to the relevant transaction.

Hence, in the case of Inheritance Tax arising on death, if a beneficiary is unable to pay their share of the tax, Revenue & Customs will then collect it from the Personal Representatives out of the remaining assets of the estate. Furthermore, the tax would then also have to be grossed up (see Section 2.4).

Conversely, a beneficiary who should have received a bequest free from Inheritance Tax under the terms of the deceased's Will could end up having to bear part of the Inheritance Tax arising when there are insufficient liquid funds left in the remaining estate.

Transferees should usually bear any extra tax arising when the transferor dies within seven years of making a gift but this rule will be overridden if Revenue & Customs finds it necessary to do so.

Example

In July 2004 Robbie gave his old friend Gary £500,000 to help him out.

Sadly, things continue to go from bad to worse for Gary and, in 2006, he is declared bankrupt.

In March 2007, Robbie dies and the earlier gift to Gary becomes chargeable to Inheritance Tax.

As Revenue & Customs will be unable to collect the Inheritance Tax due on Gary's gift from him, they will look to Robbie's Personal Representatives to pay the tax out of the assets of the estate. Instead of the original £200,000 (at 40%), however, the Inheritance Tax due on this gift will now be £333,333 (two thirds – see Section 2.10).

In short, Revenue & Customs doesn't really care who pays the tax, as long as it is collected.

This is why it will often make sense to take out term assurance to cover Inheritance Tax costs arising in the event of an unexpected early death and we will look at this further in Section 11.10.

2.8   HOW MUCH TAX IS PAYABLE?

On death, Inheritance Tax is levied, generally at one single rate of 40%, on the entire value of your estate, less certain exemptions. The most important exemptions are the nil rate band, which is £285,000 for deaths occurring during the year ended 5th April 2007, and the exemption for transfers to spouses or civil partners (see Chapter 4).

Where a lifetime transfer gives rise to an Inheritance Tax charge, the rate applying is 20%, sometimes known as 'the lifetime rate'.

Transfers to spouses or civil partners are usually tax free. Furthermore, the £285,000 nil rate band can be deducted from the total value of transfers made in the last seven years. As we shall see in Chapter 5 this is very important because it means that tax-free transfers equivalent to the nil rate band can be made every seven years.

2.9   WHAT IS YOUR ESTATE?

Your 'estate' means everything you own, including land and property, shares and securities, savings accounts, cash, antiques, jewellery, paintings, your car, your furniture and anything else which has any monetary value whatsoever.

Income arising up to the date of death must also be included (e.g. unpaid salary, accrued bank interest, etc.).

Also included in the deceased's estate will be:

i)   The net value of any assets held on their behalf in certain types of Trust (see Chapter 9),

ii) The value of any relevant 'gifts with reservation' (see Section 5.9), and

iii) The value of any assets which they elect to have included in their estate in order to avoid an Income Tax charge on a deemed benefit in kind (see Section 14.3).

For the purposes of Inheritance Tax, any non-exempt transfers of value made in the seven years prior to death will also be brought back into the deceased's estate. Reduced Inheritance Tax rates do, however, apply to gifts made more than three, but less than seven, years prior to death.

Any liabilities you have will be deducted, such as your mortgage, overdrafts, bank loans, credit card bills, amounts borrowed from friends or family (if these can be proven) and any outstanding utility bills. You may even deduct outstanding Income Tax and Capital Gains Tax liabilities!

'Reasonable' funeral expenses may also be deducted. What is 'reasonable' depends on your standard of living. (In one extreme case, the expense of a private army providing an honour guard at the funeral was deemed to be 'reasonable'.)

In other words, subject to a few technical adjustments, your 'estate' is basically your total net worth.

All of the property transferred on your death is subject to Inheritance Tax in the same way, whether it transfers under the terms of your Will, by intestacy, by survivorship (for jointly held property) or by any other means.

Tax Tip

Many people take out insurance policies to cover outstanding liabilities, such as credit card bills or bank loans, if they should pass away unexpectedly. The result of this is that these liabilities would not be deductible from the value of the estate as they were automatically settled on the taxpayer's death.

It would be far better to make provision for such liabilities by other means (see Section 11.9) and thus ensure that they are deducted from the value of your estate for Inheritance Tax purposes.

Wealth Warning

Many people assume that tax-advantaged products, such as Individual Savings Accounts (ISA's) and Personal Equity Plans (PEPs) are exempt from Inheritance Tax because they are supposedly 'tax-free'.

Unfortunately, this is not the case and **ALL** assets have to be included in your estate, regardless of their treatment for Income Tax or Capital Gains Tax purposes.

Wealth Warning

Household personal effects are generally overvalued, resulting in unnecessary overpayments of Inheritance Tax.

The valuations which most people have on their personal effects (jewellery, antiques, silverware, etc,) tend to be insurance valuations. However, the amount on which Inheritance Tax is payable should only be the open market value of the assets and this is often considerably less.

2.10   THE BASIC CALCULATION ON DEATH

To illustrate the basic Inheritance Tax calculation, let's take a look at a very simple example:

Example

Arthur has been very careful with his money all his life. At the time of his death in December 2006, his estate amounts to £2,000,000.

Arthur's Will leaves his entire estate to his son Tony, so there are no exemptions available, other than the nil rate band.

The first £285,000 of Arthur's estate is exempt from Inheritance Tax, as it is covered by the nil rate band. The remaining £1,715,000, however, is charged to Inheritance Tax at 40%, giving rise to a tax charge of £686,000!

Note that 'Grossing Up' does not apply in the above example, as Tony will bear all of the Inheritance Tax arising.

Chapter 3

Payment and Administration

3.1 MAKING THE PAYMENT

Inheritance Tax arising on death is normally due six months after the end of the month of death. Hence, in the case of Arthur who died in December 2006 (in the example in Section 2.10 above), it will be due by 1st July 2007. Personal Representatives may sometimes have to pay the tax even earlier however, as the liability is triggered when they deliver their accounts for probate purposes.

This same payment date applies to all Inheritance Tax arising on death, both on the deceased's estate itself and on gifts made within the previous seven years (see Section 5.5).

The Personal Representatives may elect for any tax arising which is based on the value of land or buildings within the deceased's estate, to be paid in ten equal yearly instalments, commencing six months after the month of death. If the property concerned is subsequently sold, however, then all of the remaining Inheritance Tax relating to that property (which has not yet been paid under the instalment system), becomes payable immediately.

Interest is charged on, and added to, payments made by instalments.

Interest is, of course, also charged on late payments under any other circumstances.

The current interest rate applying to both instalments and other late payments is 4% (one of the best interest rates in the tax system, it must be said).

Paying Tax on Lifetime Transfers

Where Inheritance Tax becomes payable on a lifetime transfer, it is due as follows:

i) Gifts made between 6th April and 30th September – Inheritance Tax is due on 30th April in the following tax year.
ii) Gifts made between 1st October and 5th April – Inheritance Tax is due six months after the end of the month in which the gift is made.

From a pure cashflow point of view, therefore, the best day to make a chargeable gift is 6th April. (This may not always fit in with the rest of your planning though!)

3.2   ACCOUNTS

The term 'accounts' in an Inheritance Tax context is somewhat different to what 'accounts' means for the purposes of most other taxes.

In most cases, the delivery of 'accounts' is satisfied by the completion and submission of:

- Form IHT200 in respect of the estate of the deceased, or
- Form IHT100 in respect of:
  o Chargeable lifetime transfers (see Section 5.2)
  o Gifts received within the seven years prior to death
  o Gifts with reservation of benefit (when the transferor has now died – see Section 5.9)

To complete form IHT200, the Personal Representatives of the estate will need to provide details of:

i) The assets of the estate and their value at the time of the deceased's death,
ii) Lifetime transfers made by the deceased within the seven years prior to death,
iii) Any relevant reliefs and exemptions claimed, and
iv) The amount of Inheritance Tax due.

Form IHT100, where relevant, must be completed by the transferor in the case of any chargeable lifetime gifts and by the transferee in the case of gifts becoming chargeable on the transferor's death: either because they were made within the seven years prior to death or because they are classed as a 'gift with reservation' (see Section 5.9).

The normal time limit for delivery of 'accounts', i.e. forms IHT100 or IHT200, as the case may be, is:

- Twelve months from the end of the month in which a chargeable lifetime transfer takes place, or
- Twelve months from the end of the month of death in all other cases.

Extended time limits may apply where the Personal Representatives had not yet been appointed on the normal due date.

3.3 EXCEPTED ESTATES

Accounts (i.e. form IHT200) are not required for 'excepted estates'.

Broadly speaking, an 'excepted estate' is one which has either:

i) A total gross value no greater then the nil rate band, or

ii) A total gross value of less than £1m and a net value, after deducting liabilities and transfers to the spouse, or to charity, of no more than the nil rate band.

The nil rate band used for this purpose depends on when death occurs:

- For deaths occurring between 6th April and 5th August where the application for grant of representation (or confirmation in Scotland) is made before 6th August: the nil rate band for the preceding tax year.
- In all other cases: the nil rate band for the tax year in which death occurs.

The gross value of the estate is the total value of all of the deceased's assets plus any 'specified transfers' and 'specified exempt transfers' within the seven years prior to death.

A 'specified transfer' is any transfer of cash, quoted shares or securities or tangible moveable property (such as paintings, jewellery or antiques), or an outright gift of any interest in land or buildings to another individual.

A 'specified exempt transfer' is a transfer which is exempt because the transferee is the transferor's spouse, a charity, a qualifying employee trust or historic building maintenance fund, or one of the other bodies covered in Section 4.8.

To be an 'excepted estate' certain other conditions must also be satisfied. Where the deceased was UK Domiciled, these conditions include:

i)   The value of 'specified transfers' within the last seven years does not exceed £100,000,

ii)   The deceased did not make any transfers within the last seven years prior to their death other than 'specified transfers' (e.g. any transfers of unquoted shares, or transfers of land or buildings to a trust or a company, within the last seven years will mean that the deceased's estate cannot be an 'excepted estate'),

iii)   The deceased's estate does not include assets held in more than one trust and the value of any assets held in trust does not exceed £100,000,

iv)   The total gross value of any foreign assets included in the estate does not exceed £75,000, and

v)   There are no gifts with reservation (see Section 5.9) to be included in the estate.

Different conditions apply for the estates of non-UK Domiciled persons.

Where the Personal Representatives of smaller estates are exempted from the requirement to produce detailed accounts (form IHT200) under the 'excepted estates' rules set out above, they must still provide some limited information to the Probate Service, or the Scottish Court Service, as the case may be.

Revenue & Customs monitor this process via information provided to them by the Probate Service or its Scottish counterpart. In some cases, they will call for a full set of accounts from these smaller estates as a 'check'.

In most cases, Revenue & Customs should now obtain any accounts for smaller estates which it wishes to examine directly from the Probate Service or the Scottish Court Service, meaning that the Personal Representatives of such small estates need only deal with the Government once. (I should think so too!)

3.4   PENALTIES

Under a new regime, applying from 22nd July 2004, penalties will now be imposed as follows:

i)   £100 for late delivery of an Inheritance Tax account (forms IHT100 or IHT200).

ii)   A further £100 for accounts delivered more than six months late.

iii) Up to £3,000 for failure to submit an Inheritance Tax account within twelve months of the due date.

iv)   Up to £3,000 for failure to notify Revenue & Customs of the variation of a disposition on death within twelve months of when such a notification is due (see Section 15.10).

The aggregate total of any penalties under (i) and (ii) above is limited to an amount equal to the Inheritance Tax actually due. These penalties may also be waived where there is a reasonable excuse for the late delivery of the account.

It is claimed that these new penalties are meant to bring the Inheritance Tax regime more in line with the penalty rules for Income Tax and Capital Gains Tax.

Funnily enough though, one of the very few 'reasonable excuses' which Revenue & Customs will usually accept for a late Income Tax Self Assessment Return is death. Surely then, as far as Inheritance Tax is concerned, everyone must have a 'reasonable excuse' for late delivery of accounts?

Sadly, in reality, I don't suppose that Revenue & Customs will see it that way. However, considering the circumstances under which Inheritance Tax arises, I really have to say that the imposition of penalties does amount to 'kicking people when they're down'!

Penalties applying to the submission of 'negligent or fraudulent' material to Revenue & Customs are no longer imposed in cases where the negligence or fraud did not actually result in any change to the amount of Inheritance Tax due.

Now, in the case of negligence, I would applaud this as a fair and sensible relaxation of the previous penalty regime. Why, oh why, however, is the Government also exempting the fraudulent? Against a background of ever-tightening regulation under anti-Money Laundering regulations and the Proceeds of Crime Act, this hardly makes any sense!

3.5   ADMINISTRATION

Inheritance Tax is administered by the Capital Taxes Office of Revenue & Customs, who may be found at:

Scotland

> Meldrum House
> 15 Drumsheugh Gardens
> Edinburgh
> EH3 7UG

England and Wales

> Ferrers House
> PO Box 38
> Castle Meadow Road
> Nottingham
> NG2 1BB

Northern Ireland

> Level 3
> Dorchester House
> 52-58 Great Victoria Street
> Belfast
> BT2 7QL

The Capital Taxes Office has its own area within the Revenue & Customs website: www.hmrc.gov.uk/cto. Inheritance Tax forms can be downloaded from: www.hmrc.gov.uk/cto/forms3.htm

They also run a helpline: 0845 30 20 900. Inheritance Tax forms can also be obtained by telephoning this number or by faxing your order to: 0845 234 1010.

Chapter 4

Exemptions and How to Maximise Them

4.1 WHAT IS AN EXEMPTION?

Inheritance Tax exemptions come in many different forms.

Some exemptions are based on value, others on the relationship between the transferor and the transferee, still others on the nature of the transferee alone and some even on the circumstances of the transferor's demise.

Some exemptions have a general application, others apply only to lifetime transfers and others only to transfers made on death.

An 'exemption' for Inheritance Tax purposes, means that a particular type, or amount, of transfer is exempt from Inheritance Tax.

This means that that particular type, or amount, of transfer can be left out of the Inheritance Tax calculation altogether.

In Chapter 6, we will look at the Inheritance Tax exemptions which apply only to lifetime transfers. In this chapter, however, we will concentrate on exemptions which apply regardless of whether the gift or transfer is made during the transferor's lifetime or on death.

In each case, there are a number of exceptions designed to prevent the exemption from being abused.

To start off with, let's look at the two most important general exemptions:

- The nil rate band, and

- The exemption for transfers to spouses or civil partners.

4.2   THE NIL RATE BAND

The nil rate band is perhaps the most important Inheritance Tax exemption for the vast majority of people. As the name suggests, what the nil rate band means is that an Inheritance Tax rate of nil is applied to the first part of your estate, which falls within this band.

The amount of nil rate band available depends on the date of death. More accurately, it depends on the UK tax year of death.

Like many other tax exemptions, the nil rate band is generally increased on an annual basis, in line with inflation. However, as is also the case with many other tax exemptions, the increase is usually only given by reference to retail price inflation.

When 'New Labour' came to power in 1997, the nil rate band stood at £215,000. In the nine-year period since then, it has been increased by a total of 32.5%, to £285,000. However, in the period from May 1997 to January 2005, house prices rose by an average of 120% nationally (141% in London).

Hence, if the nil rate band had been increased, as seems more appropriate, in line with house price inflation, rather than retail price inflation, it should have stood at £473,000 (or £518,000 if it had a London 'weighting') by last year.

Given these dramatic recent increases in property values, plus the general increase in the levels of personal wealth in the UK, what this actually means is that the Government's 'take' from Inheritance Tax is steadily increasing.

For the tax year 2004/2005, an estimated 35,000 people will pay Inheritance Tax. This is more than double the number paying the tax in the last full tax year before 'New Labour' came to power in 1997.

Furthermore, the revenue raised by the Government through Inheritance Tax on the estates of deceased persons increased by **over 50%** between 1997/1998 and 2003/2004.

How's that for stealth tax!

In his Budget statement on 16th March 2005, Chancellor Gordon Brown claimed that the latest increase in the nil rate band would "exempt 95% of all estates from this tax".

What he was referring to there, of course, was <u>current</u> deaths. When one considers the potential Inheritance Tax liabilities of people who are still working, or in the early years of their retirement, the story is very different!

In fact, the current annual take from the tax of around £2.5 billion is forecast to increase to a level of *£8 billion a year* in the near future.

The nil rate band has been set for the next four tax years as follows:

For deaths occurring:

Between 6th April 2006 and 5th April 2007:	£285,000
Between 6th April 2007 and 5th April 2008:	£300,000
Between 6th April 2008 and 5th April 2009:	£312,000
Between 6th April 2009 and 5th April 2010:	£325,000

The previous nil rate band applying in recent years has been as follows:

For deaths occurring:

Between 6th April 2005 and 5th April 2006:	£275,000
Between 6th April 2004 and 5th April 2005:	£263,000
Between 6th April 2003 and 5th April 2004:	£255,000
Between 6th April 2002 and 5th April 2003:	£250,000
Between 6th April 2001 and 5th April 2002:	£242,000
Between 6th April 2000 and 5th April 2001:	£234,000

It is important to note that each individual has their own nil rate band. I will come back to this point, and explain its significance in Inheritance Tax planning, later.

4.3   THE SPOUSE EXEMPTION

Except as noted below, all transfers of property to your spouse or civil partner are completely exempt from Inheritance Tax. This covers both lifetime transfers and transfers made on death.

Exception – Spouses or Civil Partners with Separate Domicile

Where one of you is UK Domiciled and the other is not, the general exemption for transfers between spouses or civil partners is restricted.

In this case, only the first £55,000 of transfers from the UK Domiciled spouse or civil partner to the foreign Domiciled spouse or civil partner is exempt.

There is no restriction on transfers in the opposite direction – why would there be? – such transfers would potentially increase Revenue & Customs' tax haul. They might also have foreign tax implications!

Where either spouse is deemed to be UK domiciled (see Section 2.2), they will be counted as UK domiciled in applying the above rule.

This may open up some interesting planning ideas for any married couples with mixed domicile.

Example

Mary is UK domiciled but has a large number of foreign assets. Her husband Farouk is domiciled in Tanzania, but has lived in the UK for the last 18 years and therefore has deemed UK domicile for Inheritance Tax purposes.

Mary can therefore transfer all of her foreign assets to Farouk and this transfer will be fully exempt for Inheritance Tax purposes. Farouk could then leave the UK and would automatically lose his deemed UK domicile three years later.

All of Mary's foreign assets, now held by Farouk, would then be free from UK Inheritance Tax.

"Couldn't Mary achieve the same result just by emigrating herself?" you may ask. Yes, she could, but it would be much harder for her to shed her UK domicile, whereas, for Farouk, it will be automatic.

Other Exceptions to the Spouse Exemption

The general exemption for transfers between spouses or civil partners is also restricted in a few other circumstances. The exemption may be lost where:

i) The transfer to the spouse or civil partner only takes effect after the expiry of another third party's interest in the asset or after the expiry of some other period of time.

Tax Tip

It is, however, acceptable to have a condition in your Will that your spouse or civil partner must survive you by a certain period before becoming entitled to the asset.

ii) The transfer is dependent on a condition and that condition is not satisfied within twelve months after the date of transfer.

iii) The transfer is only made as consideration for the transfer of a reversionary interest in some other property.

iv) The transfer is made into a trust, where the transferee spouse or civil partner has an 'interest in possession' (see Chapter 9) which comes to an end before the death of the donor spouse or civil partner.

For those of you who follow such things, exception (iv) was introduced with effect from 20th June 2003 to block a previously popular avoidance scheme which became the subject of the 'Eversden' case. It is possible that the proposed changes to the taxation of trusts which are currently making their way through Parliament will render this exception irrelevant for transfers on or after 22nd March 2006.

What is a Spouse?

Sounds like a daft question, doesn't it? Well, it's not – read on.

For Inheritance Tax purposes, a spouse must be your <u>legally married</u> husband or wife or your legally registered civil partner.

A 'spouse' is not specifically defined in tax legislation but, for Inheritance Tax purposes, Revenue & Customs take the view that the exemption continues to apply to any transfer between persons who are still legally married at the time of that transfer.

Unlike Capital Gains Tax, therefore, the Inheritance Tax exemption for transfers between spouses continues to apply to separated couples right up until the granting of a decree absolute.

Transfers between spouses on separation or as part of divorce proceedings will therefore be covered by the exemption if they are made before the granting of decree absolute.

Generally speaking, a couple who are legally married under the laws of another country will similarly be recognised as legally married for tax purposes in the UK.

This will even include polygamous marriages when they are legally valid in the taxpayer's country of origin. In such cases, however, the £55,000 limit, where relevant, must be applied to the cumulative value of transfers made to all of the transferor's non-domiciled spouses.

Wealth Warning

The exemption applies only to legally married couples or registered civil partners. There is no Inheritance Tax exemption for transfers to common-law partners!

Bigamists are not entitled to the exemption either.

Tax Tip

If you intend leaving most of your estate to a common-law partner then, if you can, try to get married (or enter a registered civil partnership, as the case may be) before you die. Deathbed marriages have been known to save **millions** of pounds in Inheritance Tax and it is one planning device which is almost impossible for Revenue & Customs to overturn.

4.4   DOUBLING THE NIL RATE BAND

As explained in the previous section, transfers to your spouse or civil partner are usually exempt from Inheritance Tax. However, utilising this exemption to the full is not always necessarily a good idea.

Hence, the first question I ask anyone who comes to me for Inheritance Tax planning advice is "are you married?"

This is because every married couple or civil partnership can save up to £114,000 (40% of £285,000) in Inheritance Tax for their family by following a fairly straightforward planning strategy.

All that this strategy involves is simply ensuring that the first one of the couple to die uses their nil rate band on transfers which are not made to their widow, widower or surviving civil partner.

Without this strategy, the couple is simply wasting one of their nil rate bands and thus volunteering to give the Government an extra £114,000!

Example

Remember Arthur from Section 2.10? He died in December 2006, leaving his net estate worth £2,000,000 to his son Tony. Tony ended up with an Inheritance Tax bill of £686,000.

Arthur was, in fact, a widower, and within his estate there was a property worth £285,000, which he had inherited from his wife Doris, who had died in June 2006.

Since Doris left the property to her husband and it was therefore exempt anyway, her nil rate band was never used.

What Doris should have done, instead, was to leave her property to their son, Tony. No Inheritance Tax would have been payable on her death, as her property was covered by the nil rate band.

But when Arthur died later in the year, his estate would have been worth £285,000 less, i.e. £1,715,000. After deducting Arthur's nil rate band, Tony would have had to pay Inheritance Tax at 40% on just £1,430,000. Tony's Inheritance Tax bill would thus have been £572,000, giving him a saving of £114,000.

In effect, therefore, Tony would have benefited from two nil rate bands instead of just one.

Non-Spousal Legacies

The non-spousal legacy (e.g. the one to Tony in the above example) does not need to be one specific property.

It could be a whole group of assets, or simply worded as a legacy equal to the nil rate band to be paid out of the general assets of the estate.

Tax Tip

When including a non-spousal legacy in your Will with the intention of utilising your nil rate band, it is best not to word it as a legacy of the specific sum which happens to be the current amount of the nil rate band.

What you should do instead is to draft your Will so that it includes a legacy equal to whatever the nil rate band happens to be at the time of your death.

That way, the amount of the legacy will automatically adjust in line with the nil rate band each year.

But What if You're Not That Well Off?

The non-spousal legacy strategy is pretty simple to follow when, like Arthur and Doris above, there are plenty of assets around.

The problem for most married couples or civil partnerships, however, is that they can't afford to simply give their children, or other beneficiaries, £285,000 when one of them dies.

The widow, widower or surviving civil partner will need to retain sufficient assets to support them for the rest of their life including, in most cases, the family home.

Fortunately, as we shall see in the next two sections, there are some planning strategies available to deal with this dilemma facing the moderately wealthy couple.

Further strategies specific to the family home will also be covered in Chapter 13.

4.5   THE NIL RATE BAND WILL TRUST

One method for married couples to double the nil rate band which was very popular a few years ago was for each spouse to set up a discretionary trust through their Will (see Chapter 9 for an explanation of discretionary trusts).

Assets at least equal to the nil rate band would be left to the trust. The surviving spouse would be one of the beneficiaries of the trust and, in practice, would actually retain all the benefits of ownership of the assets in the trust.

This was achieved by ensuring that the trustees exercised their 'discretion' in such a way as to ensure that the surviving spouse received all of the income from, and enjoyment of, the assets.

These schemes were even sometimes used to pass the deceased's share of the family home into the discretionary trust.

However, Revenue & Customs have recently attacked these types of discretionary trusts on the basis that they are really 'de facto' interest in possession trusts.

This means that the assets of the trust will remain in the surviving spouse's estate for Inheritance Tax purposes, rendering this planning void.

Nevertheless, the Nil Rate Band Will Trust might perhaps still work where the trust is genuinely discretionary in nature.

This would necessitate avoiding the usual 'Letter of Instruction' to the trustees stating that the surviving spouse or civil partner is to receive all income from the trust.

It would also be wise to ensure that other beneficiaries did, indeed, receive some trust income.

4.6   THE WIDOW'S LOAN SCHEME

Another, and perhaps better, method for married couples to double the nil rate band is to leave all (or most) of the assets of the estate to the surviving spouse as specific bequests, but leave a sum equal to the nil rate band to a Discretionary Will Trust.

The surviving spouse would be a beneficiary of the trust, together with other family members.

The surviving spouse ends up owing a sum equal to the nil rate band to the trust.

What they then do is to simply execute a loan agreement for this amount in favour of the trust.

When the surviving spouse subsequently dies, the amount of the loan is deductible from their estate, thus doubling the nil rate band!

This scheme, generally known as 'The Widow's Loan Scheme', has the added strength that the Capital Taxes Office of Revenue & Customs has confirmed that they accept its validity, in principle, for Inheritance Tax purposes, as long as it is done properly.

'Doing it properly' includes:

- Drafting the Will very carefully,
- Ensuring that the trust is genuinely discretionary in nature (for the time being, at least),
- Ensuring that the trustees have the power to enter into a loan agreement (instead of demanding immediate payment),
- Preparing formal loan documentation, preferably secured on property held by the surviving spouse (e.g. the family home), and
- Above all, it means getting professional advice!

Wealth Warning

This method may not work if the funds used to acquire any of the assets left to the surviving spouse had originally been given by the survivor to their now deceased spouse.

If, for example, a widower had given £500,000 to his wife three years before her death and she subsequently dies leaving just £500,000, the sum supposedly loaned to the widower under the 'Widow's Loan Scheme' will clearly have come out of his pocket in the first place. For this reason the scheme would then fail.

In less obvious cases, it may be difficult to establish what funds have passed between the spouses and hence whether the survivor had, in fact, funded the loan which they are now receiving.

To avoid these difficulties, it may make sense for the couple to equalise their estates throughout their married life.

4.7 THE DAUGHTER-IN-LAW PLAN

I am not sure how many people would follow this plan in practice but, in theory, this should work.

I will illustrate the plan with an example.

Example

Frank, a widower, is almost 90 years old. He has a huge estate which he wishes to leave to his son, Frank Junior.

Unfortunately, Frank has done no Inheritance Tax planning and now realises that relying on surviving for seven years may not be good enough.

Frank Junior is engaged to Nancy, a 30 year old, UK domiciled, singer.

However, what the family decides is that, instead of marrying Frank Junior, Nancy should marry 90 year old Frank.

Shortly after the marriage, Frank gives everything he owns to Nancy. This transfer is exempt under the spouse exemption.

A little while later, Nancy divorces Frank and marries Frank Junior. She can now (if she wishes) transfer everything to Frank Junior and it will again be exempt from Inheritance Tax under the spouse exemption.

As I said, this works in theory.

Will Revenue & Customs accept it? Like any other aggressive tax planning strategy this probably depends on how well it is done. To date, Revenue & Customs have not had occasion to challenge the validity of a marriage.

But the real problem with this plan lies in the phrase "if she wishes". What is there to stop Nancy from running off with all of the family's money?

The above strategy can easily be adapted to pass wealth from a widow to her daughter.

Now that we also have the possibility of registered civil partnerships, a similar strategy may also now be possible to pass wealth on from father to daughter or from mother to son.

4.8   GIFTS TO CHARITIES & OTHER EXEMPT BODIES

Generally, all gifts to charity are exempt from Inheritance Tax. This covers both outright gifts and transfers into a Charitable Trust. A charity is defined as 'any body of persons established for charitable purposes only'.

Wealth Warning

Foreign charities are excluded!

Gifts to certain other bodies are also exempt, as follows:

- **Gifts to Housing Associations**
  Transfers of value which are attributable to land in the UK and are made to registered social landlords are exempt from Inheritance Tax.

- **Gifts for National Purposes**
  Gifts to any of the bodies set out in Appendix E are exempt from Inheritance Tax.

- **Gifts to Political Parties**
  Gifts to qualifying political parties are exempt from Inheritance Tax. Funny that, isn't it?

  To qualify, the party must either have had at least two members elected to the House of Commons, or have received no less than 150,000 votes in total and had one member elected to the House of Commons, at the last General Election.

4.9   DEATH ON ACTIVE SERVICE

There is a complete exemption from any Inheritance Tax arising on the death of a person from wound, accident or disease contracted whilst on active military service.

A valid certificate issued by the Ministry of Defence is required in support of any claim under this exemption.

Chapter 5

Lifetime Transfers

5.1 INHERITANCE TAX ON LIFETIME TRANSFERS

In Section 2.1, we established that what triggers Inheritance Tax is not death, but any 'transfer of value'.

However, prior to 22nd March 2006 very few transfers during a person's lifetime actually gave rise to any immediate Inheritance Tax.

The reason for this seemingly contradictory position was the fact that any lifetime transfers to another individual, or to most types of trust, were treated as 'Potentially Exempt Transfers' – free of inheritance tax after seven years. We will return to this concept in Section 5.3.

From 22nd March 2006, however, the only lifetime transfers which may still be treated as 'Potentially Exempt Transfers' are those to:

- Another individual,
- A bare trust, or
- A disabled trust.

Even in these cases, it remains important to realise that 'potentially exempt' effectively also means 'potentially chargeable' (ie taxable) and most lifetime transfers are therefore potentially subject to Inheritance Tax.

Throughout this chapter, I will be referring many times to various different types of trust. The concepts involved in the various trusts will all be explained in Chapter 9.

5.2 CHARGEABLE LIFETIME TRANSFERS

As explained above, many lifetime transfers are 'potentially exempt'. Since 22nd March 2006, however, any lifetime transfers to:

- A company, or
- Any trust other than:
  - A disabled trust,
  - A bare trust, or
  - A charitable trust,

will be **chargeable (ie taxable) lifetime transfers**.

Prior to 22nd March 2006, it was generally only transfers to a company or to a discretionary trust which represented chargeable lifetime transfers.

Some readers unfamiliar with the nature of trusts may not feel that this change is particularly restrictive until I tell you that many insurance premiums represent a transfer of value into a trust. (Most of these are, however, exempt for other reasons, as we will see later.)

Chargeable lifetime transfers may be <u>immediately</u> chargeable to Inheritance Tax, depending on the cumulative value of such transfers made by the transferor within the last seven years.

Transfers of value into companies are rare and the major incidence of chargeable lifetime transfers are therefore transfers into trusts.

The amount of the chargeable transfer is arrived at by deducting any available exemptions (see Chapters 4 and 6) from the 'transfer of value'.

The amount of Inheritance Tax due is then calculated as follows:

Other chargeable transfers within the last seven years   X
PLUS
This chargeable transfer   X
LESS
nil rate band   (X)

EQUALS the amount on which Inheritance Tax is now chargeable.

Inheritance Tax on lifetime transfers is charged at half death rates, i.e. 20%.

Example

In this example, we are ignoring all exemptions and reliefs, other than the nil rate band.

Two years ago, Elvis gifted some investments worth £50,000 into a discretionary trust, thus giving rise to a Chargeable Transfer. No Inheritance Tax was payable at the time, of course, as this was well within his nil rate band.

Elvis now gifts his former home, Graceland, which is worth £350,000, into a discretionary trust (for the purposes of this example, it does not matter whether this is the same trust or not), on condition that the trust settles any Inheritance Tax arising.

The trust's Inheritance Tax liability is calculated as follows:

Previous Chargeable Transfers within last 7 years: ADD	£50,000
This Chargeable Transfer EQUALS:	£350,000
Cumulative Chargeable Transfers LESS:	£400,000
nil rate band EQUALS:	£285,000
Amount chargeable	£115,000
Inheritance Tax Payable at lifetime rate (20%)	£23,000

Alternative Scenario – with 'Grossing Up'

Note that, if Elvis had settled the Inheritance Tax himself, it would have been subject to 'Grossing Up', as follows:

Amount chargeable, as before	*£115,000*
Grossing Up factor – one quarter	*£28,750*
Grossed Up Amount	*£143,750*
Inheritance Tax Payable at lifetime rate (20%)	*£28,750*

Wealth Warning

Note that, in this example, Graceland was Elvis's <u>former</u> home. This is a very important point since, as we will see later in the guide, it is very difficult to make an Inheritance Tax-effective transfer of your current home.

Tax Tip

If Elvis was married, he could have avoided any Inheritance Tax on his gift of Graceland by first transferring it into joint names with his wife before they both jointly gifted it to the discretionary trust. Each of them would then have made a Chargeable Transfer of only £175,000. Even after taking his previous Chargeable Transfer into account, Elvis would then have been covered by his nil rate band.

Elvis's wife would also be covered by her nil rate band as long as she had not made other Chargeable Transfers within the last seven years in excess of £110,000.

Avoiding 'Grossing Up'

In the above example, we have looked at the situation where the Inheritance Tax is paid by the transferee (the Trust), as well as the situation where it is paid by the transferor (Elvis himself).

More tax is generally payable where the transferor is settling the liability. This is because the transferor is deemed to be making a gift not only of the original asset transferred, but also of the tax arising. This, in turn, is because the 'transfer of value' is once again calculated by reference to the reduction in value of the transferor's overall estate and the payment of the Inheritance Tax arising naturally increases the amount of that reduction.

The bad news here is that, in the absence of any evidence to the contrary, the transferor is always assumed to be liable for any Inheritance Tax. Hence, if care is not exercised, you may find that the value of any gifts which you make turns out to be 25% larger than you had expected!

The way to avoid this is to draw up a memorandum of your gift which stipulates that the transferee is to pay any Inheritance Tax arising. An example of a suitable memorandum is included as item 2 in Appendix D.

5.3   POTENTIALLY EXEMPT TRANSFERS

As explained in Section 5.1, many lifetime transfers are Potentially Exempt Transfers (or PETs, for short) which fall out of the inheritance tax net after a number of years.

Prior to 22nd March 2006 lifetime transfers made by an individual to any of the following were Potentially Exempt Transfers:

    i)   Another individual
    ii) A Bare Trust
    iii) An interest in possession trust
    iv) An Accumulation and Maintenance Trust
    v) A Disabled Trust

From 22nd March 2006, however, only transfers by an individual to (i), (ii), or (v) above are potentially exempt. Furthermore, the exceptions noted below still apply.

Transfers made *by* a trust are subject to different rules and we will explore these in Chapter 9.

Exceptions

The following transfers will not qualify as Potentially Exempt Transfers:

- Any transfers to your UK-Domiciled spouse or civil partner (these are fully exempt, except as noted in Section 4.3 above).

- The first £55,000 of transfers to your non-UK Domiciled spouse or civil partner (again, these are fully exempt except as noted in Section 4.3).

- Any other transfer covered by another general or lifetime exemption (see Chapters 4 and 6). (This, of course, will be of no practical consequence unless and until the transferor dies within seven years of making the transfer.)

- Any transfer which does not result in an increase in the value of the transferee's estate (see further in Section 5.4 below).

- Transfers of value caused by alterations to share capital, loan capital or other rights in most private companies.

- Deemed, as opposed to actual, transfers of value (e.g. on the cessation of a reservation of benefit on an earlier 'gift with reservation' – see Section 5.9).

- A transfer of value to a disabled trust (or, before 22nd March 2006, to an accumulation and maintenance trust) which does not consist of a transfer of property into the trust (see further in Section 5.4 below).

So What Do We Mean By 'Potentially Exempt'?

Put simply, these transfers are potentially exempt because all the transferor has to do is to survive for seven years after making the transfer for it to then become fully exempt and completely free and clear of any possible Inheritance Tax liability (subject to the Gifts with Reservation rules – see Section 5.9).

In the meantime, the transfer is treated for all Inheritance Tax purposes as if it is exempt (i.e. no Inheritance Tax is due) and only becomes chargeable if and when the transferor dies within seven years of the date on which the transfer was made. If the transferor is still alive at the beginning of the seventh anniversary of the transfer, full exemption will have been achieved.

Example

On 4th August 1999, Chuck gave £1,000,000 to his little brother Richard. Sadly, on 11th August 2006, Chuck is electrocuted whilst playing his electric guitar in a rainstorm.

The gift to Richard was a Potentially Exempt Transfer and, since Chuck survived the requisite seven years (just!), this sum is completely exempt from Inheritance Tax on Chuck's death.

Tax Tip

If Chuck had died a week earlier, Inheritance Tax would have been payable on his gift to Richard (see further in Section 5.5 below).

Hence, it is essential to have the documentary evidence to prove that the gift took place when it did. A memorandum along the lines of items 1, 2 or 3 (as appropriate) in Appendix D should suffice for this purpose.

See also Section 5.7 below regarding the timing of gifts made by cheque.

5.4   PROBLEMS WITH PETS

One little known, but potentially important, point about Potentially Exempt Transfers is that there must be an increase in the value of the transferee's estate in order for the transfer to qualify.

Furthermore, where the transferee is a disabled trust (or, for transfers before 22nd March 2006, an accumulation and maintenance trust), there must be an actual gift of property into the trust.

Any transfers which do not qualify as potentially exempt transfers as a result of failing to meet these requirements will be chargeable lifetime transfers, unless some other exemption is available to cover them.

Examples of transfers of value which do not increase the transferee's estate might include:

i) A grandparent paying their grandchild's school fees. The grandchild, whilst receiving an indirect benefit, does not enjoy any increase in the value of their estate.

ii) Paying an insurance premium on a policy held for someone else's benefit. The value of the policy remains the same before and after payment of the premium, so there is no increase in the value of the transferee's estate.

iii) A parent paying the maintenance costs for their adult child's house. The value of the house may not necessarily be increased through routine maintenance, so neither is the child's estate.

Each of these payments may, however, be exempt under the 'normal expenditure out of income' exemption (see Section 6.8).

In the first situation, the grandparent could avoid the problem by giving the necessary funds to cover the school fees to the child's parent, who would then pay the school fees themselves.

Similarly, the second situation might be rectified by giving the money to pay the premium to the beneficiary who then pays it themselves, although this does depend on who the policyholder is and whether the policy is held in trust. In practice, the position regarding insurance premiums has now (since 22nd March 2006) become rather complicated and we will therefore return to this subject in more detail in Section 11.9.

The position in the third situation above is perhaps arguable. In a case like this, there is a potentially exempt transfer to the extent that the value of the child's house is increased as a result of the work paid for by the parent. The remainder of the parent's expenditure, however, represents a chargeable lifetime transfer (unless it is covered by any other exemption).

Example

Joe's daughter, Sam, would like to have her house completely redecorated. Joe offers to get the work done at his own expense. He therefore contracts for a decorator to do the work, which is then carried out at a cost of £20,000.

Joe has therefore made a transfer of value of £20,000.

Before the redecoration work, Sam's house was worth £300,000. Immediately after the work, it is worth £308,000.

Joe has therefore made a potentially exempt transfer of £8,000 (the increase in the value of Sam's house), but the remaining £12,000 of his expenditure will be a chargeable lifetime transfer (unless covered by other exemptions).

Joe could have prevented any chargeable lifetime transfer very easily by simply giving all of the money for the redecoration work to Sam and leaving her to contract for the work and pay the bill herself.

Alternatively, if Sam had contracted for the work herself and was therefore liable for the decorator's bill, Joe could settle that bill and this would also be a potentially exempt transfer as Sam's estate increases when her liability is settled.

Either way, it is sensible for Sam to contract for the work!

Wealth Warning

If Joe were contractually liable for the work on Sam's house but he gave Sam the money to pay the bill and she settled it, this would result in a potentially exempt transfer of £20,000 from Sam to Joe, as well as the transfers already described in the example above.

If **either** of them died within seven years, this could result in additional Inheritance Tax liabilities arising.

As explained above, the requirements for a transfer to qualify as a potentially exempt transfer where the transferee is a trust are even more restrictive.

If Sam's house was held by a disabled trust for her benefit, the only way for Joe to fund the redecoration work as a potentially exempt transfer would be for him to give the trust £20,000. The trustees could then contract and pay for the necessary work.

If Joe settled the decorating bill, then this would be a chargeable transfer regardless of who had contracted for the work.

Wealth Warning

Settling a debt on behalf of a disabled trust will not qualify as a potentially exempt transfer.

5.5 DEATH WITHIN SEVEN YEARS OF A LIFETIME TRANSFER

For Capital Gains Tax purposes, death is often a very good tax-planning strategy. The same cannot be said, however, of Inheritance Tax.

Both Chargeable Lifetime Transfers and Potentially Exempt Transfers made in the seven-year period prior to death are brought back into the deceased's estate for Inheritance Tax purposes.

This applies whether any Inheritance Tax was actually payable at the time of the original transfer or not.

Subject to the Tapering provisions (see below), Inheritance Tax becomes payable at the death rate (40%) on transfers made within the seven years prior to the transferor's death. Any Inheritance Tax paid on the original transfer, however, may be deducted, so that it is just the excess which arises on death.

The additional Inheritance Tax liabilities arising are usually the responsibility of the transferees. In other words, the situation may be like this:

> "I'm very sorry to hear about your father, son, but do you remember that gift of £10,000 that he gave you two years ago? Well, I'm afraid you're going to have to pay some tax on it now."

Now do you see why I call it an 'immoral and evil tax'?

The best way to avoid unwanted liabilities falling on transferees in the event of your death within seven years is to record your

53

intention to bear any tax arising in a memorandum at the time of the gift (see item 3 in Appendix D).

Alternatively, you can make a specific bequest in your Will in respect of the Inheritance Tax falling on the transferee.

(To avoid doubt, it is probably best to do both.)

There are two problems with both of these approaches, however:

i)   The payment of Inheritance Tax arising at the time of your death from out of your estate will itself represent another transfer of value and hence 'grossing up' at full death rates will apply.
ii) The primary responsibility for any Inheritance Tax arising on death remains with the transferee. If there are insufficient funds remaining in your estate to cover the tax arising, the transferee will still have to foot the bill.

In practice, it often makes more sense for the transferee to take out term assurance on the life of the transferor in order to cover any potential Inheritance Tax arising on the latter's death.

Conversely, the transferor will often be concerned to ensure that any Inheritance Tax arising on earlier gifts does not come out of his or her estate and thus reduce the value of the net estate passing to their primary beneficiaries.

In theory, of course, the Inheritance Tax arising on transfers made in the last seven years of the transferor's life should be paid by the transferees. However, as we saw in Section 2.7, Revenue & Customs are more concerned with collecting the tax than with who gets hurt. To put matters (reasonably) beyond doubt, it is therefore wise to use a memorandum specifying the transferee's responsibility for any Inheritance Tax arising (see item 2 in Appendix D). Sadly, however, even this will not help if the transferee simply does not have the ability to pay the tax.

Tapering

Fortunately, there is some relief where death occurs more than three, but not more than seven, years after the lifetime transfer.

In these cases, the rate of Inheritance Tax arising on the death is tapered as follows:

No. of years after transfer before Death occurs:	Proportion of 40% 'Death Rate' Payable
Not more than 3	100% (=Inheritance Tax @ 40%)
More than 3, not more than 4	80% (=Inheritance Tax @ 32%)
More than 4, not more than 5	60% (=Inheritance Tax @ 24%)
More than 5, not more than 6	40% (=Inheritance Tax @ 16%)
More than 6, not more than 7	20% (=Inheritance Tax @ 8%)

Tax Tip

Thanks to the tapering provisions, Inheritance Tax starts to be saved once the transferor manages to survive just three years. Hence, even if you don't think that Great Aunt Maude stands any chance of lasting seven years, it's still worth looking at getting her to make some gifts.

Wealth Warning

Note that the reductions in the amount of Inheritance Tax payable occur on the *day after* the anniversaries of the gift, not the anniversary itself!

(Although, as we saw in Section 5.3, a potentially exempt transfer actually becomes fully exempt on the seventh anniversary of the transfer.)

In the case of Chargeable Lifetime Transfers (see Section 5.2 above), the tapering provisions could result in the final Inheritance Tax liability on death actually being less than the amount already paid.

Unfortunately, this simply means that no further Inheritance Tax is due; it does not result in any repayment.

In calculating the Inheritance Tax due on each transfer made within the seven years prior to death, any chargeable transfers in the seven years before that transfer must be taken into account.

For this reason, chargeable lifetime transfers made up to 14 years previously may therefore continue to have an impact on the Inheritance Tax arising on the transferor's death.

Hence, the calculation of the tax arising on transfers made within the seven years prior to death is almost a repeat of the calculation which we saw in Section 5.2 for a chargeable lifetime transfer, except that:

- The full death rate (40%) is used
- Tapering relief (as set out above) is applied
- The nil rate band available at the date of death is used in the calculations, rather than the nil rate band applying at the time of the transfer
- potentially exempt transfers made in the seven years prior to death must be brought into the calculation

The effect of all this is best illustrated by way of an example.

Example

As in previous examples, we will ignore any exemptions and reliefs, other than the nil rate band.

Roy, a kind, generous and rich old man, dies on 3rd December 2006. Roy had made no chargeable lifetime transfers prior to 1996 but, in the last few years of his life, he made the following gifts:

- *On 10th December 1996, he gave £200,000 in cash to the Wilbury discretionary trust.*

- *On 1st December 1999, he gave £50,000 in cash to his son George.*

- *On 13th January 2000, he gave another £100,000 in cash to the Wilbury discretionary trust. He paid £17,250 in Inheritance Tax at that time (grossing up applied).*

- *On 8th May 2002, he gave his friend Jeff some shares in the Electric Light Company Inc. At that time, these shares were worth £50,000.*

- On 3rd December 2003, he gave his friend Tom some shares in Heartbreakers.com plc, which were worth £80,000 at that time.

- On 30th August 2004, he gave his friend Bob £100,000 in cash.

The Inheritance Tax payable on Roy's death by each of these transferees is as follows:

The Wilbury discretionary trust – First Gift

Roy's first gift to the Trust in 1996 was made more than seven years prior to his death. This gift itself, therefore, will not be subject to Inheritance Tax on his death. However, because gifts to discretionary trusts are chargeable transfers, it will continue to have an impact on later gifts made in the next seven years.

George

Roy's gift to George was a potentially exempt transfer made more than seven years prior to his death.

On the seventh anniversary of that gift, 1st December 2006, the gift became fully exempt and hence it can now be completely ignored for the purposes of calculating any Inheritance Tax arising on Roy's death.

The Wilbury Discretionary Trust – Second Gift

Due to the grossing up provisions, Roy's second gift to the Trust in January 2000 was deemed to have been a gift of £117,250. As this gift was within the last seven years of Roy's life, it is pulled back into his estate for the purposes of his Inheritance Tax calculation.

Furthermore, in calculating the Inheritance Tax now due on this gift, we must also take account of his previous gift to the Trust, as that first gift was a chargeable transfer made within the seven year period prior to the second gift.

The gift to George on 1st December 1999 can, however, be ignored as this has become fully exempt.

The cumulative total of chargeable lifetime transfers made by Roy up to the time of the second gift to the Trust was therefore £317,250.

After deducting the nil rate band of £285,000 from this sum, there remains a chargeable sum of £32,250.

As the gift took place more than six, but less than seven, years before Roy's death, Inheritance Tax is chargeable at only 20% of the death rate, i.e. 8%.

Hence the Inheritance Tax charge on this gift arising on Roy's death is £2,580. As this is less than the Inheritance Tax already paid by Roy on the lifetime transfer (£17,250), no further Inheritance Tax is therefore payable.

Jeff

Roy's gift of shares to Jeff on 8th May 2002 was a potentially exempt transfer. Unfortunately, as Roy has died within seven years of making that gift, it has now become a chargeable transfer.

Both of the gifts to the Wilbury discretionary trust took place within the seven year period prior to the gift to Jeff, so the cumulative value of chargeable transfers at this point is £317,250, meaning that the nil rate band has been fully exhausted and the gift to Jeff is now fully chargeable to Inheritance Tax.

However, since the gift to Jeff took place more than four, but less than five, years before Roy's death, Inheritance Tax is only chargeable at 60% of the death rate, i.e. 24%.

Jeff therefore has an Inheritance Tax liability of £12,000 (£50,000 x 24%).

Tom

Tom really is going to be heartbroken. His gift took place exactly three years before Roy's death.

Unfortunately, Inheritance Tax tapering only begins on the day **after** the third anniversary of the gift.

Inheritance Tax is therefore payable at the full death rate, 40%.

Furthermore, the cumulative value of total chargeable transfers within the previous seven years now amounts to £367,250, made up as follows:

	£
Gift to Wilbury discretionary trust	*200,000*
Gift to Wilbury discretionary trust	*117,250*
Gift to Jeff	*50,000*
Total	*367,250*

Both gifts to the Wilbury discretionary trust are included as they both took place within the seven year period prior to the gift to Tom.

The gift to Jeff is also included as it has now become a chargeable transfer due to Roy's death within seven years.

The gift to George is not included, however, as it took place more than seven years before Roy's death and has therefore become exempt.

Tom therefore has an Inheritance Tax liability of £32,000 (40% x £80,000).

Bob

This gift took place within the last three years of Roy's life, so there is no tapering of the Inheritance Tax liability.

The cumulative value of total chargeable transfers within the seven years prior to this gift amounts to £247,250, made up as follows:

	£
Gift to Wilbury discretionary trust	*117,250*
Gift to Jeff	*50,000*
Gift to Tom	*80,000*
Total	*247,250*

The first gift to the Wilbury discretionary trust no longer needs to be included as it took place more than seven years prior to the gift to Bob.

Adding Bob's own gift to the above figure gives a total of £347,250. From this, we are able to deduct the nil rate band of £285,000, leaving Bob with a chargeable transfer of £62,250.

Bob's Inheritance Tax liability is therefore £24,900 (40% x £62,250).

Points To Note

Firstly, we can see that the total value of chargeable transfers in the last seven years of Roy's life amounts to £347,250. His nil rate band is therefore already exhausted before we even begin to look at his estate.

The next point to note is that the oldest gift in our example, which was made almost ten years before Roy's death, had a major impact on the recipients of his later gifts, despite the fact that it was made well before the critical seven-year period.

It is also interesting to note that the oldest gift within the seven-year period did not give rise to any more Inheritance Tax for the recipients of that gift. This will often be the case for chargeable lifetime transfers made more than five years prior to the transferor's death. This position may be altered, however, where there are significant amounts of potentially exempt transfers made within seven years of the transferor's death but prior to the chargeable transfer in question.

As we saw in the example, these two earlier gifts used up all of Roy's nil rate band, which had a major impact on some of the later transferees.

This was particularly unfortunate for Tom since a mere eight days delay to his gift would have meant that the first gift to the Wilbury discretionary trust would then have been made more than seven years previously. Tom's own gift would then have been completely covered by the nil rate band.

Tax Tip

The last comment gives rise an important planning point.

Where it is practical to do so, it may make sense to try to leave a seven year gap after making any large chargeable lifetime transfer before making further chargeable or potentially exempt transfers.

Naturally, of course, delaying your gifts carries other conflicting risks which you will need to weigh up.

However, a delay of eight days in order to bring the nil rate band back into play again would surely make sense!

By the time of Bob's gift on 30th August 2004, part of the nil rate band was available once more, thus giving him a lower Inheritance Tax bill than Tom on a larger value gift.

This ably demonstrates the fact that, with careful planning:

The nil rate band is effectively available to each of us not just once a lifetime, but once every seven years!

Whilst none of us know exactly when we have seven years left to go, it is also worth bearing in mind the fact that gifts in the last seven years of your life will be dealt with chronologically when you die.

Although kind old Roy cannot really be blamed for the final outcome in the example, things might have turned out fairer if he had made some of the smaller gifts first.

5.6   RELIEF FOR REDUCTION IN VALUE

Where Inheritance Tax, or additional Inheritance Tax, becomes payable on a lifetime transfer made within seven years prior to the transferor's death and the transfer consisted wholly or partly of property which has subsequently reduced in value, the transferee may claim relief from Inheritance Tax in respect of that reduction in value.

Conditions

To claim relief, these conditions must be satisfied:

i)   The property transferred must not be tangible moveable property with a predictable useful life not exceeding 50 years (e.g. a car, or any other plant and machinery), and

ii) Either:

    a)   At the time of the transferor's death the property is still held by the transferee or their spouse, or

    b)   The property has been sold by the transferee or their spouse by way of a sale at 'arm's length' to an unconnected person.

When such a claim is made, the Inheritance Tax on that particular transfer is calculated by substituting the property's market value at the 'relevant date' for the property's value at the date of the transfer.

Where the property is still held by the transferee or their spouse at the date of the transferor's death the 'relevant date' is the date of death.

Where the property has been sold in an arm's length transaction with an unconnected party, the 'relevant date' is the date of the sale.

The Inheritance Tax on any other transfers and on the deceased's estate is unaffected by this claim. This is because the value of the transferred property is reduced only for the purposes of this relief and not for the purposes of calculating cumulative chargeable transfers in any seven year period.

Example

At the time of Roy's death, Jeff still holds the shares in the Electric Light Company Inc. which Roy gave to him on 8th May 2002 when they were worth £50,000. Unfortunately, however, they are now worth only £30,000.

Jeff is pleased to discover, however, that he can claim to reduce his Inheritance Tax bill to just £7,200 (£30,000 x 24% - see Section 5.5 above for a full explanation).

Tom is also very excited at the prospect of a relief claim under these provisions as his shares in Heartbreakers.com plc fell rapidly in value after Roy gave them to him and Tom eventually sold them for just £1,000.

According to Tom's calculations, he should therefore be able to reduce his Inheritance Tax bill to just £400 (£1,000 x 40%).

However, it transpires that Tom sold the Heartbreakers.com plc shares to his son. This, therefore, was not an 'arm's length' sale to an unconnected party and Tom's Inheritance Tax bill remains £32,000 (see Section 5.5). Heartbroken again!

Points To Note

The Inheritance Tax liabilities of Bob and Roy's Personal Representatives are unaffected by Jeff's claim. (Nor would they be affected by Tom's claim if it had been valid.)

It does not matter in this case whether Tom sold his shares to his son at market value. Because he and his son are connected, Tom loses his ability to claim relief for his shares' reduction in value.

He therefore ends up with some shares which are virtually worthless and an Inheritance Tax liability of £32,000.

Sometimes it **does** pay to look a gift horse in the mouth!

Tax Tip

A transferee holding property which was transferred to them less than seven years ago and which has reduced in value since then would be wise to avoid making any transfers of that property other than:

- A sale at 'arm's length' to an unconnected person, or

- A transfer to their own spouse or civil partner

5.7 TIMING OF LIFETIME GIFTS

A gift made by cheque is deemed to be made when that cheque is cleared by the transferor's bank.

This will inevitably cause a slight delay to the date on which the gift is deemed to take place.

Whilst the delay may be slight, it could have disastrous consequences in some cases.

If the cheque clears after the transferor's death, for example, it will no longer be regarded as a lifetime gift and will form part of the transferor's estate on death. This will mean that none of the lifetime exemptions will apply, including the annual exemption and the small gifts exemption.

For the sake of certainty, therefore, it may often be worth incurring the additional cost of putting the cheque through 'same day clearing'.

5.8 EVIDENCE

When making lifetime gifts, it is vital to have the evidence to back them up.

Revenue & Customs will sometimes try very hard to get assets back into the deceased's estate in order to increase the amount of Inheritance Tax payable.

"Can you prove he gave you that painting? Are you sure he didn't just hang it in your house temporarily?"

"How do we know this money wasn't just a loan? Can you prove she didn't expect you to repay it?"

"Yes, we know your parents gave you the house, but what about the contents? There's nothing to prove that they gave them to you."

To prevent these kinds of questions from arising, it is vital that gifts are evidenced. Furthermore, it is important that the documentary evidence of the gifts is specific about exactly what is being gifted.

Appendix D contains some brief examples of memoranda recording gifts. In practice, however, it will often make sense to record further detailed information, especially details of any household contents intended to be included in a gift of property.

5.9   GIFTS WITH RESERVATION

To give something away so that it is no longer part of your estate for Inheritance Tax purposes, you really need to completely deprive yourself of that asset and any enjoyment of it.

Any purported gifts where you retain a beneficial interest in the gifted asset are ineffective for Inheritance Tax purposes and are treated as still being part of your estate.

For example, if you 'give' a painting to your son but keep it in your house then you are still enjoying that asset and it remains part of your estate for Inheritance Tax purposes.

These types of transfer are known as 'Gifts with Reservation'. This is a particular problem when looking at the family home and we will return to this subject in Chapter 13.

Broadly speaking, a 'Gift with Reservation' occurs whenever:

i)   The transferee does not obtain genuine possession and enjoyment of the gifted asset,
ii) The transferor is not excluded from the enjoyment of the gifted asset, or
iii) The transferor has some form of contractual right over the gifted asset.

We have already seen an example of (i) – the gifted painting being kept in the transferor's house.

An example of (ii) would be to give a holiday cottage to your daughter which you then use for a month each year.

An example of (iii) would be to grant yourself a lease over your own property and then transfer the freehold to your children. (This was the method used in the 'Lady Ingram' case. The third rule above was introduced when the Revenue lost that case and it applies to transfers taking place on or after 9th March 1999.)

Although you have to be excluded from the enjoyment of a gifted asset, there is a little leeway. If you give your son a painting which he keeps in his house, there is no need to wear a blindfold every time you visit him.

The strict rule is that the transferor must be 'virtually' excluded from the enjoyment of the asset. Mere incidental enjoyment of a gifted asset when making a short visit to the transferee is permitted.

Hence, if you give your daughter a house and visit her for dinner once every six months, you will not have a problem.

If, on the other hand, you stay at the house every second weekend, there will be a gift with reservation.

Unforeseen Changes in Circumstances

In the case of a property which a transferor has gifted to a relative, there will not be a gift with reservation if the transferor is forced to move back into that property due to an unforeseen change in circumstances whereby he or she is unable to care for themselves due to ill health, old age or infirmity.

This, for example, may cover the situation where a person has transferred a property to their son or daughter and some years later has to move into the property so that their family can care for them.

The move back into the property must be for the provision of 'reasonable care and maintenance' by the transferee who must also be a relative. You can't just move back in because you'd like to see a bit more of the grandchildren.

This change must also be unforeseen. If you are already ill when you make the gift, the gift with reservation rules will still apply.

What's So Bad About Gifts with Reservation?

Plenty!

Firstly, although the gift is ineffective when it comes to excluding the gifted asset from your estate, it is nevertheless still a transfer of value and could give rise to an extra Inheritance Tax charge if you die within seven years. In other words, there could be tax on the transfer **and** on the asset which is deemed to still be in your estate on death!

Some relief is given for this effective double charge but it does not entirely eliminate the problem.

Secondly, the gifted asset will also be included in the transferee's estate, thus giving rise to another possible double charge.

Thirdly, although the gift is ineffective for Inheritance Tax purposes, it will still be a disposal for Capital Gains Tax purposes. This means that Capital Gains Tax liabilities may still arise on the gift. Furthermore, the transferee may not be entitled to the same reliefs as the transferor would have been if they had retained the asset. We will look further at the potential impact of this in Chapter 12.

What Happens When The 'Reservation' Ends?

When the 'reservation' ends, a new transfer is deemed to take place and this time it is effective for Inheritance Tax purposes.

Hence, for example, if a mother gave a house to her two sons in 1999 but continues to live in it until 2007, there is deemed to be a transfer of the house in 2007.

The big problem here is that, if the transferor dies within seven years of this deemed transfer, the deemed transfer becomes chargeable to Inheritance Tax. Furthermore, the value of the deemed transfer will be the asset's value at the date the reservation ends, not the date of the original transfer.

Hence, the mother will need to live until 2014 for her transfer of the house in 1999 to be exempt from Inheritance Tax. If she should pass away before then, the value of the house when she moved out in 2007 will be brought back into her estate.

These deemed transfers are also ineligible for a number of reliefs, including the annual exemption.

5.10   WHY NOT JUST GIVE IT ALL AWAY?

After reading Section 5.3, you may be thinking that avoiding Inheritance Tax should be very simple. All you need to do is to give everything away to your family and then survive for seven years.

Well, yes, in theory, in the right circumstances, simply giving your property away during your lifetime can be an effective way to avoid Inheritance Tax.

Certainly there is no problem with giving away whatever parts of your estate you can afford to. Just remember to make sure that the gifts are Potentially Exempt Transfers and then take good care of yourself for seven years. (Or take out some term insurance to cover the Inheritance Tax risk – see Section 11.10.)

Unfortunately, however, in practice, there are a few 'catches'.

Firstly, as we have already seen, any gifts where you retain a beneficial interest are treated as still being part of your estate.

Secondly, even where a transfer appears to avoid the 'Gifts With Reservation' rules, there may be an Income Tax benefit-in-kind charge applying from 6th April 2005 if the transferor continues to enjoy the use of the asset. This charge may also apply to any future use by the donor of an asset purchased with gifted funds. (See Chapter 14 for further details.)

Thirdly, when gifting assets other than cash during your lifetime, you may be exposed to Capital Gains Tax.

Most lifetime gifts are treated like a sale at current market value for Capital Gains Tax purposes. (Here there is no problem with the family home, as it is generally exempt from Capital Gains Tax under the Principal Private Residence provisions – these are fully explained in the Taxcafe.co.uk guide *How to Avoid Property Tax*.)

Lastly, in practice, you cannot simply give all your assets away because you will need something to live off for the rest of your life! It's fine if you're happy to go and spend the rest of your days in a monastery or a nunnery, or to live off your last £285,000 (for at least seven years) but, in reality, very few people would be happy to follow such a drastic course of action.

Hence, at this point, we need to start looking at what exemptions and reliefs are available to you and how you can plan to use them to best effect.

Chapter 6

Lifetime Exemptions

6.1 ABSOLUTE EXEMPTION

There are a number of exemptions available to cover lifetime transfers.

These are absolute exemptions, not dependent on whether you survive for any particular period.

Transfers covered by these exemptions would be free from Inheritance Tax even if you were to pass away the very next day, or even on the way home from the lawyer's office.

(You may scoff, but I know of one sad, but true, case where the taxpayer was knocked down by a bus outside the lawyer's office!)

These exemptions therefore provide very useful Inheritance Tax planning tools under the right circumstances.

Sadly though, the monetary values of the exemptions covered in Sections 6.2, 6.3 and 6.5 below have remained the same since 1981. These values are long overdue for an increase since retail price inflation alone would have almost tripled them by now!

6.2 THE ANNUAL EXEMPTION

The first £3,000 of any transfers of value, which are not otherwise exempt, which each individual makes in each tax year are exempt from Inheritance Tax.

Husbands and wives have an annual exemption of £3,000 each, as do civil partners.

If the annual exemption is not used one year, it may be carried forward and can be used in the next tax year if that following year's annual exemption is fully exhausted.

Example

Stevie makes the following gifts (having never made any before):

2006/2007:	*£5,000 to his brother Marvin*
2007/2008:	*£4,000 to his brother Smokey*
2008/2009:	*£2,000 to his sister Dionne*
2009/2010:	*£5,000 to his sister Aretha*

The first £3,000 of the gift to Marvin is covered by Stevie's annual exemption for 2006/2007.

However, his 2005/2006 annual exemption is also still available, thus covering the remaining £2,000 of this gift. The gift to Marvin is thus fully exempt from Inheritance Tax.

The unused £1,000 of Stevie's 2005/2006 annual exemption is simply lost, as it cannot be carried forward another year.

The first £3,000 of Stevie's gift to Smokey is covered by his 2007/2008 annual exemption.

The remaining £1,000 of this transfer is thus a Potentially Exempt Transfer.

The gift to Dionne is fully covered by Stevie's 2008/2009 annual exemption.

Furthermore, the unused £1,000 of this exemption may be carried forward to 2009/2010.

The first £3,000 of Stevie's gift to Aretha is covered by his 2009/2010 annual exemption.

The next £1,000 is covered by the unused balance of his 2008/2009 annual exemption. The remaining balance of £1,000 is a Potentially Exempt Transfer.

Tax Tip 1

If Stevie were married or in a civil partnership, he could have avoided the Potentially Exempt Transfers to Smokey and Aretha by, in each case, first making a gift of £1,000 to his wife or civil partner who would then have gifted this sum to the ultimate recipient.

Such interim gifts to a spouse or civil partner must, however, be free of any conditions, so that the spouse or civil partner would be free to refuse to hand the gift on to the intended recipient if they so wished.

Tax Tip 2

The annual exemption may not be very large, but it is important to bear it in mind when undertaking Inheritance Tax planning.

Making best use of the annual exemption is a matter of timing. The ability to carry it forward one year gives you an effective 'second chance', but the use of the annual exemption should nevertheless be reviewed at least every other year.

A married couple or civil partnership who managed to make effective use of the annual exemption in the final few years of their lives would save around £20,000 in Inheritance Tax.

Who Benefits From The Exemption

According to Revenue & Customs, the taxpayer's annual exemption for each tax year must be applied on a strictly chronological basis.

In their view, the exemption must be utilised against any potentially exempt transfers taking place earlier in the tax year before chargeable lifetime transfers taking place later in that same tax year.

This could have some most unfortunate consequences.

Example

Brian gives £6,000 to his brother Carl on 6th April 2006. This (according to Revenue & Customs) uses up Brian's annual exemptions for 2005/2006 and 2006/2007, despite the fact that it is a potentially exempt transfer.

On 10th April 2006, Brian gives £300,000 to the Wilson Phillips discretionary trust set up for the benefit of his many nephews and nieces.

Unfortunately, this means that he has made a chargeable lifetime transfer to the Wilson Phillips discretionary trust. After deducting the nil rate band of £285,000, the remaining sum of £15,000 must be grossed up at the rate of one quarter, giving Brian an Inheritance Tax bill of £3,750.

If, instead, Brian had made his two gifts in the opposite order, his annual exemptions for 2005/2006 and 2006/2007 would have been deducted from his chargeable transfer, leaving just £294,000, or £9,000 after deducting the nil rate band. Brian's Inheritance Tax bill would then have been reduced to just £2,250, a saving of £1,500.

Revenue & Customs interpretation on this point is, however, based entirely on a flaw in the drafting of the Inheritance Tax Act 1984.

A close inspection of the Act makes it clear that what Parliament actually intended was for the annual exemption to be used first against any chargeable lifetime transfers, with any excess remaining available to cover potentially exempt transfers if they subsequently became chargeable on the transferor's death.

This difference in interpretation will affect not only those making large chargeable lifetime transfers in excess of the nil rate band, like Brian in the example above, but also the transferees calculating their own Inheritance Tax bill in the event of the transferor's death within seven years. In the latter case there will, of course, be winners and losers but, in the former case, only Revenue & Customs can be the winners!

In practice, in a situation like this, I would always advocate planning your affairs on the basis of Revenue & Customs interpretation wherever possible.

Tax Tip

Chargeable lifetime transfers should be made earlier in the tax year than any potentially exempt transfers whenever possible.

But, if you find that you are already in the position where their interpretation is putting you at a disadvantage, you should argue for the law to be applied as it was quite clearly intended by Parliament.

Simultaneous Gifts

Transfers made on the same day are treated as being simultaneous for the purposes of the annual exemption.

Any available annual exemption is divided between the 'same day transfers' in proportion to the total value of the transfers.

Example

On 9th October 2006, John gives £10,000 to his elder son Julian and £5,000 to his younger son Sean.

John has made no previous gifts in the period since 5th April 2005.

His 2005/2006 and 2006/2007 exemptions are therefore both available, enabling £6,000 of these gifts to be exempted.

Assuming the boys' cheques both clear the same day, and following Revenue & Customs' interpretation, John's annual exemptions will be divided as follows:

Julian: £6,000 x £10,000/£15,000 = £4,000
Sean: £6,000 x £5,000/£15,000 = £2,000

Julian will therefore have received a potentially exempt transfer of £6,000 (£10,000 - £4,000) and Sean will have received a potentially exempt transfer of £3,000 (£5,000 - £2,000).

Taking this point in conjunction with Section 5.7 above, one can imagine transferees racing each other to the bank!

6.3   THE SMALL GIFTS EXEMPTION

In addition to the annual exemption, there is also a general exemption for outright gifts of up to £250 to any one person each tax year.

This exemption applies to any number of such 'small gifts' to separate persons each year.

Again, a husband and wife or two civil partners may each utilise this exemption separately in their own right.

Wealth Warning

The small gifts exemption only covers gifts of <u>up to</u> £250. Unlike the annual exemption, it does not cover the first part of a larger gift. Hence, a gift of £251 is not covered by this exemption at all.

It should also be noted that the exemption has to cover all gifts to the same person in the whole tax year.

Furthermore, this exemption cannot be used in conjunction with the annual exemption.

In other words, it is not possible to exempt gifts totalling £3,250 to the same person by using both exemptions together.

6.4   USING THE ANNUAL AND SMALL GIFTS EXEMPTIONS EFFECTIVELY

It is possible to combine these two exemptions in order to exempt a number of gifts to different family members.

Used on a cyclical basis, it will also be possible to even out any unfairness.

Example

Chris and Debbie have three sons, Scott, John and Gary, and wish to pass as much wealth on to them as they can by using their annual and small gifts exemptions.

On 5th April 2007, Chris gives Scott £6,000. This is covered by his annual exemptions for 2005/2006 and 2006/2007.

On the same day he also gives £250 each to John and Gary and these gifts are covered by the small gifts exemption.

Note that care would need to be taken here if other gifts had also been given to the sons earlier in the tax year – e.g. birthday and Xmas presents. Arguably, however, these other gifts would be covered by the 'habitual gifts out of income' exemption.

At the same time, Debbie gives John £6,000, which is covered by her annual exemptions for 2005/2006 and 2006/2007, and gives £250 each to Scott and Gary.

The next day, 6th April 2007, Chris and Debbie each give £3,000 to Gary. Both of these gifts are covered by their 2007/2008 annual exemptions. Chris and Debbie also each give £250 to Scott and £250 to John.

In the space of 48 hours, Chris and Debbie have managed to give their sons a total of £20,000, which is completely exempt from Inheritance Tax. If they should be unfortunate enough to die within seven years, this simple strategy will save the family £8,000.

*(**NB:** you may notice that Gary has received £250 less than his brothers. This can be evened out again in later years.)*

6.5   GIFTS IN CONSIDERATION OF MARRIAGE

It's an expensive business when the kids get married, but at least it does provide an extra opportunity to do some Inheritance Tax planning.

Gifts made in consideration of marriage are exempt from Inheritance Tax up to the following limits:

- Parents: £5,000
- Grandparents, Great-Grandparents, etc: £2,500
- Bride to Groom or Groom to Bride: £2,500
- Other Donors: £1,000

All of the above limits apply on an individual basis and the relationships referred to must be to one of the parties to the marriage.

Hence, for example, the groom could receive £5,000 from each of his parents, plus £2,500 from each of his grandparents and £1,000 from all of his aunts and uncles and the bride could receive the same from her family.

Alternatively, the bride's family could make their gifts to the groom or the groom's family could make their gifts to the bride.

Additionally, within this same exemption (and within the same overriding limits as set out above), gifts could be made into a trust for the benefit of:

- The bride and/or groom
- Children of the marriage
- Future spouses of the children of the marriage
- A future spouse of either party to the marriage
- Children of any subsequent marriage of either party to this marriage and future spouses of those children

Gifts in consideration of marriage must be made on or shortly before the marriage in order to fall within the exemption.

The gifts must be fully effective when the marriage takes place. For example, "I give you my property at Valotte on condition that you marry my daughter."

Where the gifts exceed the limits shown above, the excess may be covered by the annual exemption, if available.

Otherwise they will become Potentially Exempt Transfers unless made to a Trust.

A 'parent' for this purpose will include the parent of an illegitimate child, adopted child or step-child. The children of the marriage will also include children legitimated by marriage or adopted by the husband and wife jointly.

As explained in Section 1.6, all of the above applies equally to civil partnerships.

6.6 MAINTENANCE OF FAMILY

Anything you do for the maintenance of your 'family' is exempted from being a transfer of value for Inheritance Tax purposes.

This is just as well since, otherwise, every time you bought the weekly groceries you would be at risk of causing an Inheritance Tax liability!

This covers expenditure for the maintenance of your spouse or civil partner, plus any expenditure for the maintenance, education or training of the following persons:

- A child of either you or your spouse (or civil partner) who is either under 18 or still in full time education or training on the last 5th April prior to the time of the relevant expenditure.

- Any other child who is not in the care of a parent and is under 18 on the last 5th April prior to the time of the relevant expenditure.

- Any other child who has been in your care for a substantial period and was still in full time education or training on the last 5th April prior to the time of the relevant expenditure.

Your 'child' for the purposes of this exemption includes a step-child, adopted child or illegitimate child.

One major absentee from this list, however, is your unmarried partner and hence, technically, any expenditure for the maintenance of a common-law co-habiting partner would be a transfer of value.

Thankfully, however, such expenditure can probably generally be covered by:

- The 'Normal Expenditure Out Of Income' Exemption (see Section 6.8) below, or

- The general exemption for 'arm's length' transactions between unconnected persons (see Section 2.1), since your unmarried partner is not deemed to be a 'connected person and most 'transfers of value' in an unmarried couple are simply domestic cost-sharing arrangements.

Even so, it does still present a potential problem.

6.7 DEPENDENT RELATIVES

This same exemption also extends to expenditure which represents a reasonable provision for the care or maintenance of a dependent relative.

A 'dependent relative' for this purpose is:

i) Your widowed, separated or divorced mother or mother-in-law.

ii) Any other relative of yours or your spouse's who is incapacitated by old age or infirmity, as a consequence of which they are unable to maintain themselves.

By concession, an unmarried mother may also be included under heading (i) above, as long as she is genuinely financially dependent on the donor, even if she does not qualify as 'old or infirm' under heading (ii).

'Old' is usually taken to mean the male state retirement age, i.e. 65.

It can be seen that sexism is alive and well and living in the UK tax legislation. I wonder when we will see a case being taken to the European Court of Justice demanding equal treatment for widowed, separated or divorced fathers?

Revenue & Customs should, for example, accept that renting a property for your elderly and financially dependent relative to live in represents reasonable provision for their maintenance.

They will not, however, accept buying a property for them and transferring it into their name to give them added security, as 'reasonable care or maintenance'.

This exemption is generally only relevant when a child pre-deceases one of their parents, but it does happen.

6.8   NORMAL EXPENDITURE OUT OF INCOME

Lifetime transfers of value are exempt to the extent that it can be shown that:

i)   they are part of the normal, habitual, or typical, expenditure of the transferor,

ii) taking one year with another, they are made out of income (i.e. not out of capital), and

iii) the transferor is left with sufficient net income to maintain his or her usual standard of living.

This is an extremely useful exemption, since, unlike the annual exemption, there is no financial limit to the amount which can be covered by this exemption if the transferor can afford it.

The amount of gifts or other expenditure involved does not need to be exactly the same every year, as long as it is part of a regular pattern.

All of the following might potentially be covered as long as they meet the three tests set out above:

- Giving your son £10,000 every year.

- Giving your granddaughter all of your ICI dividends every year.

- Paying your nephew's school fees.

- Buying your brother a new car every three years.

- Passing all of the income which you receive from a trust each year over to your elderly father.

- Paying a monthly life assurance premium on a policy in favour of your daughter.

The last example above involves a life assurance policy. The Inheritance Tax consequences, and tax planning opportunities, surrounding life assurance policies and life insurance policies are a complex subject in their own right. Furthermore, since many policies are written in trust, the subject has become even more complex as a result of the current proposed changes to the Inheritance Tax treatment of trusts. We will therefore return to this subject in more detail in Section 11.9.

Maintaining Your Usual Standard of Living

It has been suggested that the Capital Taxes Office (the Revenue & Customs department responsible for policing Inheritance Tax) does not generally question the validity of gifts out of income if they do not, in total, exceed one third of the transferor's net annual after tax income.

Nevertheless, I imagine they would still scrutinise any case where they had reason to think otherwise!

In some circumstances, the transferor might reasonably gift a far greater proportion of his or her income and still maintain their usual standard of living, e.g. a very wealthy person with a very frugal lifestyle.

It is generally accepted that this test is met if the transferor making the normal, habitual, expenditure is left with sufficient income to maintain his or her usual standard of living **on average**.

I have, however, met the 'chicken and egg' situation where Revenue & Customs have argued that the transferor's modest standard of living arose **because** of the expenditure in question. To avoid this argument, there will clearly need to be some surplus income remaining.

What Is Income?

The first point to note is that Revenue & Customs regard 'income' for the purposes of this exemption as net after tax income.

Furthermore, not everything which is treated as 'income' for Income Tax purposes will be regarded as 'income' for the purposes of the exemption. (Yet another example of Revenue & Customs having their cake and eating it!)

There are, for example, cases where the proceeds of sale of company shares may be treated as income for Income Tax purposes. This result often occurs as a result of specific statutory provisions relating to employee shares. The underlying nature of this 'income', however, would remain capital and hence this would not be 'income' which could be relied upon for the purposes of the 'normal expenditure out of income' exemption.

For a self-employed transferor, 'income' for the purposes of the exemption would generally be based on the results shown in the transferor's accounts.

Hence, 'income' will be arrived at after deducting items such as depreciation and business entertaining, even though these are not allowed for Income Tax purposes. As stated above, however, the full Income Tax charge will need to be deducted from the accounts income in order to arrive at the net after tax income available for the purposes of the exemption.

Habitual Gifts

Establishing a gift as being part of your normal, habitual expenditure is a question of fact.

The matter will be determined by looking at the particular facts of each individual case and considering the actual behaviour of the transferor over a number of years.

Revenue & Customs will usually consider expenditure to have become normal, or habitual, when it has been made three times, with the intention of continuing to make further similar payments.

It is, however, possible to establish that a gift has become part of your normal, habitual expenditure even if you should die after only one such gift.

This is because the exemption will still apply if it can be shown that it was the transferor's intention to make the gift regularly on an habitual basis.

A contractual commitment to make regular payments will usually be accepted as evidence of an intention to make the expenditure part of the transferor's normal pattern of expenditure. In the absence of such a commitment, some other documentary evidence of the transferor's intentions is advisable.

Tax Tip

Establishing an intention to make a gift on an habitual basis will require some evidence to prove it. For example, if you intend paying your niece's school fees on a regular basis, it would be wise to write a letter to the school confirming this fact.

If you should then unfortunately pass away soon after paying the first set of fees, the letter will confirm that this payment was intended to be normal habitual expenditure and thus exempt from Inheritance Tax (as long as the other requirements set out above are also met).

Wealth Warning

To be covered by this exemption, the relevant gifts or expenditure must be maintained on a regular basis.

Hence, you must be sure to keep making your 'habitual' gifts every year (or such other period as is your habit). Unlike the annual exemption, there is no scope for carrying this exemption forward!

The Danger Of Irrelevance

Naturally, where the gifts concerned are made directly to another individual, this all only becomes relevant when the transferor has died within seven years of making the gifts concerned since, otherwise, the gifts will be potentially exempt transfers in any case (see Section 5.3).

Unfortunately, what this means in practice is that the true status of these transfers is generally never established until after the transferor's death, leaving a great deal of uncertainty for their beneficiaries.

It is vital, therefore, to maintain appropriate records of your normal expenditure out of income throughout your lifetime, to assist your executors in establishing the correct position when dealing with your estate after your death.

6.9 TRANSFERS ALLOWABLE FOR INCOME TAX OR CONFERRING RETIREMENT BENEFITS

'Transfers of value' which are made for the purposes of a trade, and hence are allowable for Income Tax, are exempt from Inheritance Tax.

This exemption also extends to payments securing pension or other retirement benefits for:

i) any employee of the transferor, who is not otherwise connected with the transferor, or
ii) the widow, widower or dependants of a person within (i) above.

Chapter 7

The Tax Benefits of Business Property

7.1 INTRODUCTION

Where the appropriate conditions are satisfied, relief from Inheritance Tax is available on the transfer of relevant business property or agricultural property.

As a result, it is now possible to pass on most family businesses free from Inheritance Tax.

Care must be exercised, however, as there are a great many pitfalls awaiting the unwary!

These reliefs apply, in principle, to both lifetime transfers and transfers on death, although, as we shall see in Section 7.13, there are a few more conditions to be met in the case of lifetime transfers.

In many cases, where available, the relief is given at 100%, meaning that the transfer of the business or agricultural property escapes Inheritance Tax altogether.

In those cases where relief is given at a rate less than 100%, the relief is given before applying any other exemptions (such as the annual exemption or the nil rate band).

Where relief is available at 50%, this will therefore effectively double the value of these other exemptions.

Example

Cliff has an industrial building worth £582,000 on which business property relief is available at the rate of 50%. He wishes to transfer the building to the Marvin-Welch discretionary trust. This will be Cliff's first chargeable lifetime transfer.

After business property relief at 50%, the chargeable transfer is reduced to £291,000. Cliff's annual exemptions for the current and previous years are still available. Deducting these (at £3,000 each) leaves a chargeable transfer of £285,000, which is covered by Cliff's nil rate band.

Note that, in the above example, there is a risk that Inheritance Tax liabilities will arise if Cliff dies within seven years of making this transfer. We will return to the subject of business property relief on lifetime transfers in Section 7.13.

Technically, no actual 'claim' is required, as these reliefs apply automatically when the relevant conditions are met. In practice, however, one does still have to 'claim' that the conditions have been met.

Trusts

These reliefs also apply to the tenth anniversary and exit charges applying to trusts (see Chapter 9). Naturally, the trust will need to meet all of the necessary conditions, including the minimum ownership period (see Section 7.11). In practice, this means that the trust will generally need to hold any business or agricultural property for at least two years before passing it on to a beneficiary in order to obtain the relief.

7.2   WHEN IS BUSINESS PROPERTY RELIEF AVAILABLE?

Business property relief (sometimes known as BPR for short) is available on transfers of business property which meet each of the following three conditions:

i)   The business concerned is a qualifying business (see Sections 7.4 to 7.7),

ii) The asset itself is relevant business property (see Section 7.8), and

iii) The asset has been owned by the transferor for at least the relevant minimum period (see Section 7.11).

7.3 JUST HOW USEFUL IS BUSINESS PROPERTY RELIEF?

Let's make no mistake about it, in my opinion business property relief is the single most useful Inheritance Tax relief available.

There is absolutely no financial limit to the amount of business property relief which a taxpayer may claim where the qualifying conditions are met.

business property relief could potentially be used to completely exempt an estate worth hundreds of millions of pounds from Inheritance Tax.

An obvious, and vital, piece of Inheritance Tax planning is therefore to maximise the value of any assets qualifying for business property relief within your estate. We will come back to this in Section 7.16.

But business property relief isn't just for those with an existing business. The relief provides a useful mechanism to give Inheritance Tax exempt funds to family and friends, as we shall see in Section 7.19. There are even some types of investments which may qualify for business property relief, as we shall see in Section 7.20.

Furthermore, it generally takes just two years for assets to achieve exemption through business property relief, which is considerably better than the seven year waiting period for potentially exempt transfers.

Sadly, however, it is all too easy to lose business property relief by failing to meet the qualifying conditions at the appropriate time.

There are some particularly nasty pitfalls to watch out for with business property relief. In fact, not only is the relief very easy to lose, but this also has a tendency to happen at just the sort of point in life when Inheritance Tax planning is becoming most important.

There is also the problem that some quite normal commercial structures will leave the business owner with business property relief at just 50% on their most valuable asset when they could so easily have had 100%.

Given the importance of this relief and the comparative ease with which it can be lost, we will therefore now take a long and detailed look at the relevant qualifying conditions. Some of this gets quite technical but is important for anyone wanting to benefit from what is arguably the most powerful way to avoid inheritance tax.

7.4 QUALIFYING BUSINESSES – BASIC PRINCIPLES

For this purpose, any business is a 'qualifying business' as long as it is being carried on with a view to profit and does not consist wholly or mainly of dealing in securities, stocks or shares or land and buildings, nor of making or holding investments (except in the case of the holding company of a trading group).

This may not initially sound too restrictive but, as we shall see, the definition of what constitutes 'making or holding investments' can be a great deal broader than what one might normally think.

Despite this, however, Lloyds underwriters generally qualify for at least some business property relief. The businesses of 'market makers' or 'discount houses' on the Stock Exchange will also generally qualify.

What Is A Business?

Case law suggests that a business will exist where at least some of the following six tests apply to the activity being undertaken:

i) The activity is a 'serious undertaking earnestly pursued' or a 'serious occupation'.

ii) The activity is 'an occupation or function actively pursued with reasonable or recognisable continuity'.

iii) The activity has 'a certain measure of substance as measured by the value of supplies made'.

iv) The activity was 'conducted in a regular manner and on sound and recognised business principles'.

v) The activity is 'predominantly concerned with the making of supplies to consumers'.

vi) The goods or services supplied 'are of a kind which, subject to differences in detail, are commonly made by those who seek to profit by them'.

Where some or all of the above tests are satisfied, the activity will constitute a business and will generally qualify for business property relief purposes unless it falls under one of the statutory exclusions outlined above.

The Importance Of The Profit Motive

Nevertheless, even though it may be accepted that a business exists, the intention to make a profit remains essential. The profit motive requirement means that businesses like stud farms or the business activities of artists or authors may sometimes be ineligible for the relief.

Tax Tip

Preparing a credible business plan would provide valuable supporting evidence that you had a reasonable expectation of making a profit from your business.

A documented annual review of the plan will also be useful, as the 'profit expectation' test must be met at the time of the eventual transfer.

Note, however, that a business plan will not help you if it clearly bears no resemblance to your actual behaviour in respect of the business.

7.5   PROPERTY INVESTMENT OR LETTING BUSINESSES

Unfortunately, as so often seems to be the case in UK taxation, property investment or letting businesses are generally not accepted by Revenue & Customs as being qualifying businesses for the purpose of business property relief.

The Revenue & Customs view is that the mere holding of investment property and collection of rent does not constitute a business for business property relief purposes. (Although this does not seem to stop Revenue & Customs from collecting Income Tax on the profits generated from this 'non-business' activity!)

Sadly, Revenue & Customs' view is supported by the fact that it was specifically stated that the letting of land would not qualify for business property relief during the parliamentary debates when the relevant rules were first enacted.

Doubtless, those of you with property letting businesses will think that this is unfair. This is certainly what the executor of a certain Mrs Burkinyoung thought in 1995 when he made a claim for business property relief on the furnished flats which Mrs Burkinyoung had been letting out on assured shorthold tenancies.

Unfortunately, when the case got to Court, the judge decided otherwise, holding that Mrs Burkinyoung's properties were only investments and did not constitute a 'business' for Inheritance Tax purposes.

It also turns out that it would not have helped the Burkinyoung family if the late Mrs Burkinyoung had instead been letting out commercial property. In another Inheritance Tax case, business property relief was also denied where the deceased's business consisted of letting out small industrial units. Once again, the judge held that the lettings amounted to the mere holding of investments.

Ancillary Services

That same judge went on to say that the provision of security services, heating or cleaning services as part of the terms of the lease would still not be sufficient, in his opinion, to create a qualifying business. The judge felt that these services would be merely incidental to the holding of investments, even though he acknowledged that such services would constitute a qualifying business if provided independently of the letting business.

Tax Tip

Separating out ancillary services into a separate business may provide landlords with some scope to get business property relief on at least part of their business.

In a later case, property maintenance services were also added to the list of ancillary services which would be regarded as merely incidental to the holding of investments. Again, therefore, it might be helpful to separate these out into a separate business.

Does Size Matter?

You may think perhaps that the reason the cases referred to above were lost may be that the letting businesses concerned were too small. Sadly, this is not the case since, in yet another case, a company letting out more than 100 properties was still not regarded as having a qualifying business.

Furnished Holiday Letting

I don't know where they get these judges from or why it is that they persist in regarding property letting as an easy and completely passive way to make a living. Nevertheless, as the law stands, it appears that the only type of investment properties which are likely to attract business property relief are furnished holiday lettings (as explained in the Taxcafe.co.uk guide *'How to Avoid Property Tax'*).

Qualifying furnished holiday letting is usually accepted to be a 'business' for Inheritance Tax purposes, as long as the lettings are short-term and the owner (or his or her employees) was substantially involved with the holidaymakers' activities.

In Conclusion

Apart from furnished holiday letting, therefore, investment property is unlikely to qualify for business property relief and you will generally need to be using property in some sort of qualifying trading business in order to be able to claim the relief.

7.6   OTHER BUSINESSES EXPLOITING LAND

A great many businesses involve some form of 'exploitation of land'. This is a legalistic term to cover the type of situation where the use, by customers, of land and buildings is essential to the nature of the business. In other words, providing the use of land or buildings to the customers is a vital component of the business.

When it comes to claims for business property relief whenever there is some 'exploitation of land' involved in the business, difficulty sometimes arises when Revenue & Customs perceive the income from the business to be derived from the use of the land rather than the provision of services. In these cases, Revenue & Customs will often attempt to argue that the business consists merely of the 'holding of an investment'.

The best defence against this argument from Revenue & Customs is to show that the business income is derived mainly from the provision of services or sale of goods and not from any form of rent or other payment for the use of land.

Let's now take a look at how the 'exploitation of land' argument has been interpreted for business property relief purposes in some specific types of business.

Property Development

Whilst dealing in land and buildings does not qualify for business property relief purposes, a property development business will qualify and the land and buildings held as trading stock by that business will be covered by business property relief.

Stately Homes

Stately homes open to the public may be covered by business property relief.

In one case, a claim for business property relief was upheld by the court when just 78% of the property was open to the public. Despite the fact that 22% of the property was closed to the public, the whole property qualified as it had to be viewed as a single asset and, furthermore, the entire exterior was important to the paying public's enjoyment of the property.

The implication here is that any building of which more than 50% is used for the public's enjoyment, as part of a commercial enterprise, might qualify for business property relief.

This would surely also extend to private museums and other similar enterprises, as long as the 'profit motive' (see Section 7.4) is present.

(All is not lost where less than 50% of the property is used for business purposes, however, as we shall see in Section 7.9.)

Bookies

The courts have held that an on-course bookmaker's pitch qualified for business property relief.

Caravan Parks

Caravan parks have occupied a lot of the courts' attention when it comes to business property relief and, to date, there have been five major cases on the subject. So far, the score is Revenue & Customs 3 – Taxpayers 2.

In essence, the taxpayers lost the cases where the majority of income came from site fees or pitch fees (which are basically a form of rent), but won the cases where the majority of income came from the provision of other services or the sale of caravans.

Most recently, the long and tortuous case of *George & Loochin (Stedman's Executors)* was eventually decided in favour of the deceased's executors when it reached the Court of Appeal. This case concerned a caravan park where a major proportion of the business income comprised site fees for the storage of caravans and mobile homes on the park. However, the saving grace for this caravan park was the fact that 72% of those fees were absorbed by overheads, mainly the upkeep of the common parts of the park.

Nevertheless, Revenue & Customs still argued that the site fees represented income from the 'exploitation of land' and that the caravan park business was thus tantamount to the mere 'holding of an investment'.

Thankfully, the judge in the Court of Appeal stated that the holding of property as an investment was only one component of the business and did not prevent it from qualifying for business property relief. He also stated that he found it difficult to see why an active family business of this kind should be excluded from business property relief just because a necessary component of the business was the holding of land.

This last judgement tells us a few things:

- An 'active' business should qualify for business property relief.

- Caravan parks are very much a 'borderline' case, as they are partly concerned with the exploitation of land.

- You get a better quality of judge in the Court of Appeal.

But seriously, any business which involves some element of 'exploitation of land' runs a risk of not qualifying for business property relief.

Other Businesses & General Guidelines

As well as caravan parks, other business which might be classed as 'borderline' for business property relief purposes would include:

- Residential care homes.
- Hostels, guest houses or hotels with long-term residents.
- Businesses providing shooting or fishing rights.

The common thread in all of these businesses is the fact that providing the use of land or buildings is a vital component of the business. This is what is meant by the phrase 'exploitation of land'.

The key to obtaining business property relief in any case where the 'exploitation of land' is present is to ensure that the majority of the business income comes from the provision of services and not from the mere 'exploitation of land'.

We will look further at the issue of how to determine what constitutes the majority of the business income in the next section.

Life Interests in Land

The cases where difficulty has arisen due to the 'exploitation of land' argument all involve taxpayers who actually owned that land. Naturally, this meant that their estate was extremely valuable, which is why the business property relief claim was so important.

It has been established, however, that a taxpayer who only held a 'life interest' in land could not be held to have a business which consisted of 'making or holding investments'. That taxpayer's business therefore qualified for business property relief, which was very useful since, as we shall see in Chapter 9, there are some cases where the full value of the underlying assets over which the deceased had a life interest has to be included in their estate.

This gives rise to a possible tax planning mechanism which might ensure that a business which could potentially fall foul of the 'exploitation of land' problem would qualify for business property relief.

Let's say that a married man owns such a business, let's say a caravan park for the sake of argument.

The married man leaves a life interest in the park to his wife, with the remainder to his children. On his death, the transfer of the park to his wife is covered by the spouse exemption.

On the widow's subsequent death, the life interest in the park would be covered by business property relief and hence, in this way, the couple have by-passed the whole exploitation of land argument.

Wealth Warning

This plan is based on a 22 year-old Capital Transfer Tax case which was only won in the Court of Appeal on a 2-1 majority.

It is therefore not impossible that this decision could be overturned in a later case!

Furthermore, if not structured correctly, business property relief may only be available at 50% on the life interest. (Although, even this is surely better than nothing.)

7.7 WHAT DOES 'WHOLLY OR MAINLY' MEAN IN PRACTICE?

As stated above, a business will not qualify for business property relief if it consists 'wholly or mainly' of 'dealing in securities, stocks or shares or land and buildings, or making or holding investments'.

Naturally, however, it follows that whilst it cannot consist 'wholly or mainly' of these activities, it can still consist 'partly' of them.

But how much?

Quite simply, 'wholly or mainly' means 'at least 50%'. "50% of what?", I hear you ask. Case law has sometimes, though not exclusively, interpreted the 50% test as relating to net profits. To be on the safe side, however, I would suggest trying to ensure that the business consists of qualifying activities to the extent that these account for over 50% of each of the following:

- Turnover (i.e. sales)
- Gross profit
- Net profit
- Proprietor's time
- Employees' time
- Assets employed in the business (but see below)

However, as we have seen already, land employed in the business may be regarded in a number of ways.

Hybrid Businesses

It is important to remember that what is required for business property relief purposes is that the business consists 'wholly or mainly' of qualifying business activities. If the 'wholly or mainly' test is met then the whole business will qualify for business property relief, including those parts of the business which are not themselves qualifying activities.

This has important Inheritance Tax planning implications as it means that business property relief may be available in respect of an investment business component which represents a minority element of a qualifying business.

Example

Ray and Dave run a property business, Kink Properties, in partnership together.

Kink Properties derives around 75% of its income from property development and the remainder from property letting.

Whilst Revenue & Customs would argue that part of the business amounts to the non-qualifying activity of holding investments, the main part of the business, property development, represents a qualifying activity. Kink Properties therefore qualifies for business property relief.

Furthermore, the whole of the Kink Properties business will qualify, including the investment properties.

To get relief on the whole value of the business, it is important to ensure that all of the assets held by the business are actually used in the business. A completely unrelated quoted shareholding might be regarded as a non-business asset, for example, and would thus be ineligible for relief.

There is an important distinction between business assets used in a non-qualifying part of the business (like Ray and Dave's investment properties), which do attract relief, and assets which are not business assets at all (like those unrelated quoted shares) which are excluded from the relief.

Assets excluded from relief are known as 'excepted assets' and we will return to this concept again in Section 7.9.

7.8 RELEVANT BUSINESS PROPERTY

The following types of property may qualify for business property relief:

Relief at 100%:

i) An interest in a qualifying unincorporated business (i.e. a sole trade or profession, or a share in a partnership).

ii) Unquoted shares in a company which is carrying on a qualifying business.

iii) Unquoted securities (i.e. not shares – e.g. loan stock) in a company carrying on a qualifying business which, either alone, or together with other unquoted shares or securities, give the transferor control of that company.

Relief at 50%:

iv) Quoted shares or securities in a company carrying on a qualifying business which, either alone, or together with other quoted shares or securities, give the transferor control of that company.

v) Assets held personally by the transferor, but used wholly or mainly for the purposes of a qualifying business carried on by a company under the transferor's control, or a partnership in which the transferor is a partner (or was prior to death in the case of transfers on death).

vi) Assets held in an interest in possession trust on behalf of the transferor and used wholly or mainly for the purpose of his or her own qualifying business.

Some Definitions:

Partnership

A partnership includes a Limited Liability Partnership (or 'LLP').

Unquoted

'Unquoted' means not listed on a recognised Stock Exchange. However, shares traded on the Alternative Investment Market (AIM) or the unlisted securities market (USM), are specifically treated as unquoted for business property relief purposes.

Shares traded on either tier of the American NASDAQ are regarded as quoted, as are shares traded on the European EASDAQ. In general, any stock market recognised by the laws of the country in which it is situated will usually be regarded as a 'recognised stock exchange' and shares traded there will therefore be treated as quoted.

The legislation seems to refer only to whether the shares or securities themselves are quoted. Revenue & Customs' notes, however, refer to a 'quoted company'. This will seldom make any difference but there does remain the question of how to treat unquoted classes of shares or securities issued by a company which has a stock market quotation for another class of shares or securities. On a strict interpretation of the legislation, I would argue that these continue to be 'unquoted', but it's not a point which I would like to rely on.

Control

The first important point to note about headings (iii) and (iv) above is that it is only shares or securities (as appropriate) which actually contribute to the transferor's control of the company which will qualify for business property relief.

Hence, for example, a shareholder who controls a quoted company by means of voting Ordinary Shares will not be entitled to business property relief on non-voting Preference Shares held in the same company.

It also follows that very few securities (e.g. loan stock, etc.) will qualify for business property relief.

'Control' is generally taken to mean that the transferor is able to control over 50% of the voting powers on all questions affecting the company as a whole. A transferor holding 50% of the voting shares plus the right to a casting vote will also have 'control'.

In deciding whether the transferor can control the requisite proportion of voting power, we can include:

- Shares held by their spouse.
- Shares transferred by them or their spouse to a charity, or other exempt body, after 15th April 1976 and still held by the transferee body at any time within the last five years.
- Shares in which they or their spouse have an 'interest in possession'.

Control need only exist before the relevant transfer. The availability of business property relief is unaffected by whether control is lost as a result of the transfer in question. (Although, of course, subsequent transfers may be affected.)

7.9 WHAT IS THE VALUE OF A BUSINESS?

For business property relief purposes, the value of an unincorporated business is made up of the whole value of all of the assets of the business, including goodwill, less any business liabilities.

The assets and liabilities of the business are all those items which would need to be taken into account in order to ascertain a value for the whole business.

Whilst business liabilities (like trade creditors, for example) need to be deducted from the value of the business, money loaned to the business does not need to be deducted.

Conversely, however, money owed to a transferor by their own business cannot be included as an additional asset in a business property relief claim.

Property on which business loans are secured cannot be included as part of the value of the business (unless, of course, the property is also used in the business).

As mentioned in Section 7.4, Lloyds Underwriters may qualify for business property relief. As in many other fields of taxation, however, special rules apply to these businesses.

Excepted Assets

The general rule is that business property relief is not available on the value of an asset which:

Has neither

a) been used wholly or mainly for business purposes for the period of two years prior to the transfer, or the period since acquisition, if less;

Nor

b) is required for the future use of the business.

In the case of property falling under heading (v) in Section 7.8, however, the above rule is revised so that, in order to qualify for business property relief, the asset in question must have been either:

a) Used for the purpose of the business of the partnership or company throughout the two years prior to the transfer, or

b) Replaced a similar previous asset (see Section 7.12) and the two assets taken together were used in the relevant business for a combined total period of at least two years within the five year period prior to the transfer.

Remember, however, as discussed in Section 7.7, the asset only needs to be used in the business.

In the case of a 'hybrid business' qualifying under the 'wholly or mainly' rule, the asset might be used in a non-qualifying component of the business and could still qualify for business property relief.

Buildings – Partial Business Use

In Section 7.6, we saw that a building used at least 50% for business purposes would qualify for business property relief as a result of the 'wholly or mainly' rule.

In many cases, however, a smaller proportion of a building may be used for business purposes.

Examples might include:

- A dentist or doctor using part of their home for an office, waiting room and surgery.

- A shopkeeper using the ground floor of their three storey house as shop premises.

In cases like this, Revenue & Customs will, by concession, permit a business property relief claim in respect of the business portion of the property provided that this portion is used exclusively for business purposes.

This applies to claims under headings (i), (v) or (vi) in Section 7.8.

7.10 BUSINESS PROPERTY RELIEF FOR SHARES AND SECURITIES

In Section 7.8, we examined the conditions which need to be satisfied before shares or securities may qualify for business property relief.

However, just because the shares or securities do, in principle, qualify for business property relief, this does not mean that the whole value of those shares or securities qualifies.

In order to calculate the available business property relief, it will be necessary to take into account any 'excepted assets' held by the relevant company.

The definition of 'excepted assets' for this purpose is the same as the general definition given in the previous section (not the revised one for transfers under heading (v)).

Example

Tommy owns 60% of the share capital in Pinball Limited, a trading company operating amusement arcades.

The company has total assets valued at £1m, net of liabilities.

However, this includes £300,000 in cash held in a deposit account which is surplus to the company's business requirements and not used in its trade.

The total value of Tommy's shares is £600,000. However, 30% of the company's value is attributable to a non-business asset (the surplus cash). Hence, Tommy's business property relief must be restricted to £420,000, leaving £180,000 (or 30%) chargeable to Inheritance Tax.

There are several important points to note about this example:

Goodwill

In the above example, we ignored the value of goodwill. Any goodwill in the company's business would be a trading asset and would therefore increase the proportion of the shares eligible for business property relief.

For example, if the company had trading goodwill worth £200,000, the total value of its assets would then be £1.2m. The £300,000 of surplus cash would then represent just 25% of the company's assets and Tommy's business property relief would be increased accordingly.

Having said that, of course, since Tommy's 60% shareholding would now be worth £720,000, the ineligible portion would remain the same (25% x £720,000 = £180,000).

This is because, in our simple example, we are assuming that the value of the company shares is the same as the total value of all of its net assets. This simplistic approach will not always be the case however.

Valuing Shares

When valuing company shares it is necessary to take account of goodwill and <u>all</u> of the company's liabilities. There is no exclusion here for money loaned to the company and all of the company's tax liabilities will also need to be taken into account.

Valuing shares is sometimes a highly complex exercise and the subject is worthy of an entire book in its own right.

To establish what <u>proportion</u> of that value is based on excepted assets, however, we need to follow different principles; namely the principles outlined in the previous section regarding the valuation of a business.

Cash On Deposit

Just because a company has cash on deposit, this does not necessarily make it an excepted asset. The question is whether that cash is surplus to the company's business requirements.

In a case like Pinball Limited, it will often be possible to argue that at least some proportion of the cash is required for working capital. Exactly what proportion will depend on the circumstances of each individual case.

Cash which is held by a company for a specific and identifiable business purpose may be included as a business asset.

Example

Johnny owns San Quentin Limited, a company which he originally formed to own and operate a nightclub, 'The Ring Of Fire'.

In August 2006, San Quentin Limited sells The Ring Of Fire for £1m. The company keeps the money on deposit because Johnny is actively looking for a new nightclub which San Quentin Limited can buy. Sadly, however, Johnny dies before the company can buy the new nightclub.

Johnny leaves all his San Quentin Limited shares to his son Sue. Thankfully, full business property relief is available on the shares because the cash held on deposit was earmarked for a specific business purpose.

This example is based on a real case (but with different names – especially the boy named Sue) which the taxpayer's executors won.

In another case, however, a similar claim was denied when the executors claimed that surplus funds were being held pending a suitable business opportunity. The court felt this was too vague and that cash on deposit could only be counted as a business asset when it was required for a palpable business purpose.

Hence, in Johnny's case, if he had decided that he'd had enough of the nightclub business and was looking around for some other investment opportunity, the business property relief would have been denied.

Tax Tip

The key to maintaining full business property relief on the shares in a company holding surplus cash is to have an identifiable business requirement for that cash. This should be documented in business plans, cashflow projections, director's board minutes, etc.

Other Investments

Other short-term investments held by the company might be eligible for inclusion as business assets if the same rationale as set out above regarding surplus cash can be established.

Alternatively, as we saw in Section 7.7, the company may have a 'hybrid business', and the investments might therefore be business assets in their own right.

Revenue & Customs will now accept that the holding of investments by a company may often be part of its normal business activities, although they will still attack cases where they perceive that the company is simply being used as a repository for non-business assets in order to artificially increase the amount of business property relief available.

7.11   THE MINIMUM HOLDING PERIOD

To qualify for business property relief, the relevant property must have been owned by the transferor for a minimum of two years prior to the transfer.

There is an exception to this requirement where the property had replaced other qualifying property (see Section 7.12) and both assets taken together had been owned by the transferor for at least two years out of the five-year period preceding the transfer.

This effectively provides a form of rollover relief for business assets for Inheritance Tax purposes.

When a widow or widower inherits business property, the ownership period for this purpose includes the ownership period of their deceased spouse.

Additionally, the minimum ownership period requirement is ignored when two successive transfers of the same property take place within two years and:

i)   the earlier transfer did qualify for business property relief,

ii) the second transfer would otherwise qualify for business property relief, and

iii) at least one of the two transfers occurred on death.

7.12   REPLACEMENT BUSINESS PROPERTY

The replacement of relevant business property by other relevant business property has been referred to a couple of times in the preceding sections.

Broadly, this means that on a disposal of the original business property, the same value was reinvested in new qualifying business property.

Provided that all of the other necessary rules are met, business property relief may still be available even when more than one replacement has taken place. Hence, in the preceding sections, where we refer to 'the two assets taken together', this could also apply to three or more assets, each of which replaced their predecessor.

Where a taxpayer relies on a replacement in order to qualify for business property relief, the amount of business property relief available is generally restricted to the amount which would have been available had the replacement not taken place.

For the specific purposes of this rule, however, the following changes are disregarded:

- The formation, alteration or dissolution of a partnership.
- The acquisition of a business by a company controlled by the former owner of that business (a.k.a. an 'incorporation').

7.13 EXTRA RULES FOR LIFETIME TRANSFERS

Where business property relief applied at the time of a lifetime transfer and the transferor then dies within seven years, there are some extra conditions which must be satisfied in order for the business property relief to also then apply at the time of the transferor's death.

The conditions are:

i) The transferee must continue to own the original transferred assets throughout the period from the date of the original transfer to the date of the transferor's death or, if earlier, the date of the transferee's own death.

ii) The original transferred assets must continue to be relevant business property for business property relief purposes at the end of the period in condition (i) above.

In applying condition (ii) above, it is generally necessary for the assets to be qualifying business property in the transferee's hands at the time of the earlier of the transferor or transferee's death.

This does not apply however, if the original assets were shares or securities which were either:

a) quoted at the time of the original transfer, or

b) unquoted throughout the period covered by condition (i).

Wealth Warning

Where a transferee holds unquoted shares, these will cease to be relevant business property if the company obtains a quotation.

This could result in a 40% Inheritance Tax bill if the transferor dies within seven years of the original transfer.

Where the transferee retains part of the original asset transferred at the end of the period covered by condition (i) then business property relief continues to apply to that part, as long as condition (ii) is also satisfied.

Furthermore, the transferee may retain their business property relief entitlement if they dispose of the original assets and acquire replacement assets (as defined in Section 7.12). The following further conditions must be met in order for the transferee to retain business property relief entitlement in these circumstances:

a) The replacement assets must be acquired within three years of the transferee's disposal of the original assets.
b) Both the transferee's sale of the original assets and their acquisition of the replacement assets must take place on 'arm's length' terms (see Section 2.1).
c) The whole consideration received on the sale of the original transferred assets is expended in acquiring the replacement assets.
d) The transferee must own the replacement assets at the time of their own death if they predecease the transferor. In other cases, they must generally own the replacement assets at the time of the transferor's death but this rule does not apply where the transferor's death occurs within the 'allowed period' – see below.
e) Apart from the 'allowed period', either the original transferred assets or the replacement assets must be owned by the transferee throughout the period from the original

transfer to the date of the transferor's death or, if earlier, the date of the transferee's death.

f) The replacement assets must be relevant business property in the transferee's hands at the date of the transferor's death or, if earlier, the date of the transferee's death. (Except as noted below.)

The Allowed Period

The three year period under condition (a) above begins when the transferee enters a binding contract to sell the original transferred assets. Fortunately, it is also only necessary for them to enter, but not necessarily complete, a binding contract to acquire the replacement assets within the requisite period. (There's more on binding contracts coming up in Section 7.15.)

This period, which is known as the 'allowed period', can also extend after the transferor's death, so that the replacement may take place up to three years after the transferor dies.

For these purposes, condition (f) above is amended so that the replacement assets need to be relevant business property in the transferee's hands at the time that the transferee acquires them.

The wording of the legislation governing condition (d) seems to suggest that only one replacement is allowed under these circumstances, unlike other 'replacements', as considered in Section 7.12.

Tax Tip

What all this means is that, if you receive qualifying business property in a gift from someone else, you may find yourself with an Inheritance Tax bill if you sell that property within seven years.

However, if you can wait at least four years before selling the gifted property, you will have the opportunity to restore your business property relief by acquiring replacement business property if your benefactor should pass away unexpectedly.

One last point on replacement assets following a lifetime transfer – an acquisition of qualifying agricultural property (see Section 7.21) will qualify as a replacement asset for these purposes.

7.14 LIFETIME TRANSFERS OF BUSINESS PROPERTY BECOMING CHARGEABLE ON DEATH

If the transferee loses the business property relief on a transferred asset then Inheritance Tax will become payable if the transferor should die within seven years of the original transfer.

Additional Inheritance Tax may also be payable on a transferor's death when the transferred asset only qualifies for business property relief at 50%.

In both cases, any other available reliefs, such as the annual exemption, may of course be taken into account.

Where the original transfer was a chargeable lifetime transfer (e.g. to a trust), only that transferee will be affected by any loss of business property relief.

However, where the original transfer was a potentially exempt transfer, the loss of business property relief will mean that the whole of the transferor's estate must be recalculated on the basis set out in Section 5.5, but without the business property relief originally claimed on the transfer.

Example

Brian owns an unquoted trading company, Satisfaction Limited.

In June 2006, he gives shares in the company worth £1m to the Wyman discretionary trust. This is Brian's first transfer of value for over seven years. Whilst it is a chargeable lifetime transfer, it is covered by business property relief, meaning that no Inheritance Tax is payable at this stage.

In February 2007, Brian gives another £1m worth of shares to his son Mick.

In March 2007, Brian gives £100,000 in cash to his nephew Keith.

In May 2009, Satisfaction Limited is floated on the stock exchange and becomes Satisfaction Holdings PLC. Sadly, the ensuing celebrations take their toll on Brian and he is found dead the next morning.

Brian's lifetime transfers to the Wyman discretionary trust, Mick and Keith must now all be brought into account for Inheritance Tax purposes.

Furthermore, business property relief is no longer available on the transfers to the Wyman discretionary trust and Mick.

The £1m transfer to the Wyman discretionary trust is now fully chargeable. After deducting the nil rate band of £325,000 for deaths occurring during 2009/2010 and the £3,000 annual exemptions for 2005/2006 and 2006/2007, the remaining £669,000 is chargeable at 40%, giving the trust an Inheritance Tax bill of £267,600.

However, for the purposes of working out any Inheritance Tax on other transfers made by Brian in the last seven years, the chargeable lifetime transfer to the Wyman discretionary trust is deemed to still be at its original value after business property relief, i.e. Nil.

Hence, Brian's 2009/2010 nil rate band, as well as his 2005/2006 and 2006/2007 annual exemptions, are all still available in computing the Inheritance Tax on the £1m gift to Mick which now also becomes chargeable. Mick's Inheritance Tax bill is therefore also £267,600.

Mick's gift, however, does exhaust Brian's nil rate band and 2005/2006 and 2006/2007 annual exemptions so the whole £100,000 of the gift to Keith is chargeable to Inheritance Tax at 40%, giving him a bill of £40,000.

Poor Keith never even got any Satisfaction Limited shares and yet the simple fact that the company was floated on the Stock Exchange has cost him £40,000!

This example shows what a dangerous combination gifts of shares and company flotations present. Not only did the flotation lead to an Inheritance Tax cost for the transferees holding shares, but it also had an adverse effect on another transferee.

Things could have been worse. If Brian had made his gift to Mick before his gift to the Wyman discretionary trust, the trust's Inheritance Tax bill would have been £400,000. As things stand, at least Brian's nil rate band and two of his annual exemptions could effectively be used twice.

Tax Tip

In view of the danger that business property relief might be lost following a lifetime transfer, it is better to make chargeable transfers of qualifying business property first before potentially exempt transfers of qualifying business property.

7.15 HOW TO PRESERVE YOUR BUSINESS PROPERTY RELIEF

For anyone with a qualifying business, business property relief is an incredibly valuable relief.

The trouble is that you still need to qualify for the relief at the moment at which a transfer takes place. That moment may be death in many cases and this carries some inherent problems.

Firstly, it is generally pretty unpredictable when this will be.

Secondly, it may be some time after you cease to be interested in running a business. Most people will want to retire at some point and, unfortunately, this will often result in the loss of their business property relief.

Selling Up

As soon as you have a binding contract for sale, you are, for Inheritance Tax purposes, no longer regarded as owning the asset being sold. Instead, you are regarded as owning a right to the sale proceeds.

That right is generally not a qualifying asset for business property relief purposes.

Hence, at one stroke of a pen, you can lose your business property relief and substantially increase your family's Inheritance Tax bill in the event of your death.

Example

Eddie owns an unquoted trading company, Cochran Limited. The company is Eddie's only asset so, as things stand, Eddie has no need to worry about Inheritance Tax.

Eddie gets a great offer from a French company, Aznavour S.A., to buy Cochran Limited for £10m. He decides to accept the offer so he flies to Paris, takes the Metro to Aznavour S.A.'s lawyer's office and signs a binding contract to sell his company.

Leaving the office, Eddie looks the wrong way crossing the street and steps in front of a bus.

Inheritance Tax bill: £3,886,000!

This example is based on a true story!

OK, this is perhaps an extreme example but it does demonstrate the ease with which business property relief can be lost and the dire consequences which may result. (And it is based on a true story, after all.)

An entrepreneur like Eddie might well have been intending to reinvest his sale proceeds in a new business venture and hence might have regained the protection of business property relief within a few weeks by virtue of the 'replacement property' rules which we examined in Section 7.12.

Eddie might have considered taking out some insurance to cover the Inheritance Tax risk during this short interval.

When a taxpayer who has sold a qualifying business within the last three years gets a little more warning of their demise, the 'replacement property' rules might provide an answer.

Tax Tip

The protection of business property relief will generally be maintained if the taxpayer reinvests all of the sale proceeds from qualifying business property into new qualifying business property within three years.

Exceptions To The Loss Of Business Property Relief On Sale

A binding contract for sale will not result in a loss of business property relief if the contract is:

a) For the sale of an unincorporated business to a company which is to carry on that business where the purchase consideration is wholly or mainly shares or securities in that company.

b) For the sale of shares or securities in a company for the purposes of reconstruction or amalgamation.

Liquidation And Winding Up

Business property relief is lost on a company's shares if the company is in liquidation or in the process of being wound up.

There is an exception to this, however, if the winding up is being carried out as part of a scheme of corporate reconstruction or amalgamation (e.g. a company reorganisation or a merger of two companies).

Retirement

Business property relief is lost as soon as a partner retires from a qualifying partnership business.

Any capital which the retired partner leaves in the business is simply regarded as a loan and is ineligible for business property relief.

The way to avoid this problem is for the partner to continue in partnership, but with a very small profit share. (Remaining in partnership does, of course, have commercial implications which should also be considered.)

When a sole trader retires there is no business so there can be no business property relief. The answer here may be to take on a partner and then, at a later date, to 'semi-retire' – i.e. reduce to a very small profit share in the same manner as described above.

A taxpayer owning qualifying shares or securities in a trading company can happily retire without any loss of business property relief as their position depends on their shareholding and not on whether they actually participate in the company's business.

Tax Tip

Incorporating the business prior to retirement may sometimes be a good way to preserve business property relief.

Buy-Out Clauses On Death: A BIG NO-NO!

It is common business practice for business partners to enter into an agreement whereby their executors will sell their partnership share to the surviving partners in the event of their death.

Similar agreements are also often used by shareholder directors of unquoted companies whereby their executors sell their shares back to the company or to their fellow directors in the event of their death.

Whilst these agreements make a good deal of commercial sense, from a business property relief perspective they represent a disaster waiting to happen. This is because, at the moment of death, a binding sale contract will come into force and the estate will not hold relevant business property, but, as we saw above, will instead hold a non-qualifying right to sale proceeds.

To avoid this problem, it is essential to avoid any form of agreement which may form a binding contract on the death of a partner or director.

Cross Options

A far better alternative is to use cross options.

In other words, the business partners should enter into an agreement whereby, in the event of a partner's death, their executors will have an option to sell the deceased's partnership share and the surviving partners will have an option to buy it.

Similarly, private company directors would enter into an agreement whereby, in the event of a director's death, their executors will have an option to sell the deceased's shares or securities in the company and either the company itself or the surviving directors will have an option to buy them.

To be on the safe side, it is wise to ensure that the options are 'non-coterminous'. Broadly, this means that the option to purchase and the option to sell may only be exercised at different times. (E.g. the deceased's executors must exercise the option to sell within six weeks of the deceased's death and the surviving business partners, or directors, must exercise the option to purchase more than six, but less than twelve, weeks after the deceased's death.)

Revenue & Customs have specifically confirmed that this approach is acceptable in the case of a business partnership and there is no reason to suppose that the same principles would not be equally valid in the case of unquoted company shares or securities.

Using cross options will therefore preserve any business property relief entitlement whilst also satisfying the original commercial objective of allowing the deceased's share of a business to be 'bought out'.

Other Approaches For Partnerships

Revenue & Customs have also confirmed that the following other methods for dealing with a deceased partner's share of a business will preserve any business property relief entitlement available:

- Partnership ceases on death, partnership assets to be realised and deceased partner's estate receives appropriate share of proceeds.

- Partnership continues and deceased's estate represents the deceased.

- Partnership share falls into deceased's estate with surviving partners having an option to purchase at either a valuation or an agreed formula-based price.

- The deceased's partnership share accrues to the surviving partners but the deceased's estate is entitled to payment at either a valuation or an agreed formula-based price.

- Cross options (as explained above) which must be exercised within a set period following the partner's death.

7.16 MAXIMISING BUSINESS PROPERTY RELIEF

Where an individual owns and controls a qualifying trading company, the whole value of that company will effectively be fully exempt from Inheritance Tax.

As that individual nears the end of their life, therefore, it would make sense to ensure that the value of the company is maximised.

Furthermore, any assets held personally by the individual and used in the company's business would only qualify for 50% business property relief.

Again, it might make sense to ensure that these were held in the company.

The potential savings which could be achieved can be illustrated by way of an example.

Example

Madge is a very wealthy and very old woman. Amongst her many assets is her unquoted trading company, Ciccone Ltd. She also owns a CD pressing plant used by the company.

Ciccone Ltd is currently worth £4m. This value takes account of the fact that the company owes £2m for the purchase of new equipment and also has a bank overdraft of £1m.

The CD pressing plant is worth £10m.

If Madge were to die with things as they stand, her Personal Representatives would be able to claim business property relief as follows:

	£
Ciccone Ltd: £4m @ 100%	*4,000,000*
Pressing Plant: £10m @ 50%	*5,000,000*
TOTAL	*9,000,000*

Realising that she isn't immortal after all, Madge decides to undertake some Inheritance Tax planning.

She uses £3m out of her substantial private wealth to subscribe for further new shares in Ciccone Ltd, thus enabling the company to pay off the debt for the new equipment and the bank overdraft.

She also transfers the pressing plant into the company. (If done correctly, this can be done free of both Capital Gains Tax and Stamp Duty Land Tax.)

Ciccone Ltd will now be worth £17m and, after just two years, the whole of this value will be covered by 100% business property relief.

The overall value of Madge's estate will be virtually unchanged (subject to Wealth Warning 1 below). However, this simple piece of planning will save her family £3,200,000 in Inheritance Tax!

Note that it will take two years for Madge's new shares in Ciccone Limited to qualify for business property relief. The transfer of the pressing plant, however, will provide an immediate saving.

Wealth Warning 1

Although the transfer of the pressing plant in the above example can be carried out free of Capital Gains Tax, there could be adverse consequences in the event of an ultimate sale of the property by the company.

The Capital Gains Tax consequences of transferring property into a company are covered in depth in the Taxcafe guide *Using A Property Company To Save Tax*.

Wealth Warning 2

The Inheritance Tax planning undertaken by Madge worked because her company was in debt and was using the pressing plant in its business.

If, on the other hand, she had injected so much capital into the company that it had a surplus in excess of its usual trading requirements, there would have been a restriction on her business property relief under the 'excepted assets' rules (see Section 7.10).

The restriction would have operated by reference to the amount of the 'non-trading' surplus as a proportion of the company's total net assets.

If the surplus were large enough, the company might even have failed the 'wholly or mainly' test (see Section 7.7) and thus ceased to qualify for business property relief altogether!

7.17 SHELTERING INVESTMENTS WITH BUSINESS PROPERTY RELIEF

business property relief on company shares may also be reduced, or possibly lost altogether, if a non-trading asset, such as an investment property or quoted share portfolio, were transferred into the company. (Such a transfer may also give rise to Capital Gains Tax liabilities.)

However, as we have already seen, there would nevertheless remain the possibility of arguing that a 'hybrid business', qualifying under the 'wholly or mainly' principle (see Section 7.7) existed, so that the investment property or quoted share portfolio might be sheltered from Inheritance Tax within the trading company.

But how far can we push this?

If investments are simply being dumped into a trading company, Revenue & Customs are unlikely to accept the 'hybrid business' argument and, as we saw in Section 7.7, may argue that the company is simply being used as a repository for non-business assets.

The important distinction to remember is that investments can only be sheltered within a trading company qualifying for business property relief if they form a part of the company's business.

A random cobbled together collection of non-trading investments will not be good enough.

The best way to make use of the trading company 'shelter' would therefore be to build an investment 'arm' to the company's business over a number of years. It would be vital to ensure that this part of the business remained comfortably less than 50% of the company's overall business, bearing in mind the various possible tests set out in Section 7.7.

To maintain full business property relief on the company's shares, its investment business 'arm' would need to be an integral part of the company's overall business and it is important to reflect this in the company's records, including management accounts, director's board minutes, cashflow projections, etc.

Example

After making the transfer of the pressing plant and subscribing for new shares which we saw in Section 7.16, Madge begins to make some quoted investments within Ciccone Limited. She runs the entire enterprise as a single business, ensuring that management accounts, directors' board minutes and other company documentation all record the fact that the investment arm is an integral part of Ciccone Limited's business.

A few years later, the total value of the company is £30m, including £10m worth of investments and trading assets worth £20m.

By building the investment portfolio within Ciccone Limited instead of privately, Madge has reduced her Inheritance Tax exposure by £4m.

A similar approach could also be taken to shelter investments from Inheritance Tax within a trading partnership.

It would, however, probably be difficult for a sole trader to achieve the same result as Revenue & Customs would probably view them as having two businesses, one qualifying for business property relief and one not. If, however, the 'investments' were an integral part of the same business, this problem might be overcome.

Wealth Warning

Under the 'wholly or mainly' test for business property relief purposes, a company could still qualify with just under 50% of its activities being non-trading activities.

For the purposes of a number of Capital Gains Tax reliefs, including taper relief, however, the company will lose its trading status if just 20% of its activities are non-trading activities. This may have significantly adverse consequences for the company's shareholders. The criteria to be used for this 20% test would broadly follow the same headings examined in Section 7.7 and are thus extremely wide.

In Madge's case above, for example, Ciccone Limited would have ceased to qualify as a trading company for Capital

Gains Tax purposes as soon as the investments represented 20% of the company's value.

The rate of taper relief which Madge would get on a sale of her Ciccone Limited shares would then begin to fall from 75% and would be reduced to just 40% ten years after the company's trading status was lost.

With just 40% taper relief, Madge could be left with a taxable gain of up to £18m on a sale of the company, giving her a potential Capital Gains Tax bill of £7.2m.

If Madge had kept the investments in Ciccone Limited down to just under 20% of the company's overall value, she would still have enjoyed taper relief of 75% on a sale of those shares.

As in many cases, the taxpayer is left having to weigh up the comparative merits of Inheritance Tax savings against potential Capital Gains Tax costs. We will see more examples of this in Chapter 12.

The best compromise solution in this situation is clearly to try to keep within the 20% rule which applies for Capital Gains Tax purposes, although this does diminish the potential Inheritance Tax savings somewhat.

7.18   BUSINESS SUCCESSION PLANNING

From a tax perspective, the last thing a dying person should do is sell their business!

The day before the sale, the business would have been completely covered by business property relief and available to be passed on to their family free of Inheritance Tax.

The day after the sale, the sale proceeds would be completely exposed to Inheritance Tax, resulting in the loss of up to 40% in Inheritance Tax.

This is on top of any Capital Gains Tax which arose on the sale. (The Capital Gains Tax could also be avoided if the family sold the business shortly after the original owner's death.)

In practice, unfortunately, and much to Revenue & Customs' delight, it will often be necessary to sell the business before the owner's death. Very often, a large proportion of a business's value can be lost when its proprietor dies. After all, it is better to let Revenue & Customs take 40% of a great deal than to deny them their share of not very much.

Ideally, business succession planning is something which should be looked at much earlier on, when the original proprietor is still hale and hearty and looking forward to a well-deserved retirement.

However, if a 'deathbed sale' type of situation does arise, one way to avoid the pitfalls described above would be to sell the business in exchange for unquoted shares in a trading company. Full business property relief would then be preserved.

7.19   BUSINESS PROPERTY RELIEF FOR SMALLER SHAREHOLDINGS

It is also worth remembering that **any** shareholding in an unquoted trading company qualifies for 100% business property relief. This includes shares in companies listed on AIM or the USM (more of which later).

The problem is that when one considers the generally volatile nature of unquoted shares, combined with the minimum two-year holding period for business property relief, putting your wealth into these types of assets just to avoid Inheritance Tax is a pretty risky business.

Nevertheless, under the right circumstances, it is certainly something to consider. Let's look at an example.

Example

Noel wins a substantial sum on the National Lottery. "Great," his brother Liam says, "how 'bout helpin' me out with me business then?"

Noel agrees to give Liam £100,000 to help get his new business started.

However, if Noel simply gives Liam the money, this will be a Potentially Exempt Transfer and if Noel dies within seven years, it will have to be brought back into his estate.

So, what Noel does instead is to subscribe for shares in Liam's company, Wonderwall Ltd. After just two years, the Wonderwall Ltd shares will qualify for business property relief and Noel can then give them to Liam free from Inheritance Tax. (As long as Liam keeps the shares until Noel's death, or his own, if earlier, or at least seven years if they both last that long.)

7.20   THE AIM EXEMPTION

I have said it enough times but I know you think it's too good to be true, so here it is again:

Shares traded on the alternative investment market (AIM) are eligible for 100% business property relief.

In other words, Inheritance Tax really is still voluntary and here's how to avoid volunteering in five easy steps:

    i)   Sell everything you've got unless it already qualifies for business property relief or Agricultural Property Relief at 100%.
    ii) Put £285,000 on deposit.
    iii) Buy an annuity to give yourself sufficient guaranteed income to get by on.
    iv) Put everything else into a portfolio of AIM shares.
    v)   Survive two years.

Step (iii) is optional but probably sensible.

Too drastic for you? Perhaps, but the key point to remember is that, although AIM shares are classed as 'unquoted' for most tax purposes, including business property relief, they are still listed and traded and are thus effectively liquid assets.

Are they risky? Well, yes, all investments are risky, but AIM shares have outperformed the FTSE in recent years.

Furthermore, the risk is reduced if you invest in a portfolio of shares.

And you can afford a bit of risk can't you. Think about it – if you lose, say 20% of your investment but save 40% in Inheritance Tax, your family are still better off aren't they?

So, the full five step plan may not be for you, but there could still be a place for some AIM shares in your Inheritance Tax planning strategy.

Wealth Warning 1

Whilst AIM shares are eligible for business property relief in principle, it remains important that the companies in which you invest are themselves carrying on qualifying businesses.

This will, however, include AIM companies with a 'hybrid business' which passes the 'wholly or mainly' test (see Section 7.7).

Wealth Warning 2

If your AIM shares get a full listing your business property relief will be lost (unless you control the company).

Having said that, if this does happen, you will probably have made a nice profit on the deal so it wouldn't be all bad would it?

7.21 AGRICULTURAL PROPERTY RELIEF

Agricultural Property Relief applies in a broadly similar way to business property relief. The following types of property may be covered:

i) Agricultural land or pasture
ii) Woodlands

iii) Buildings used for the intensive rearing of livestock or fish
iv) Farmhouses, cottages and other farm buildings
v) Stud farms

Property under (ii) to (iv) must be occupied on a basis ancillary to property also occupied under (i) or (v). A separate Inheritance Tax deferral relief is available for woodlands in the UK which do not qualify for Agricultural Property Relief.

Buildings used to grow indoor crops, such as mushrooms for example, may qualify in their own right without the need for any additional agricultural land.

Agricultural Property Relief applies to agricultural land in the UK, the Channel Islands or the Isle of Man. It is given at rates of 50% or 100%, depending on the exact circumstances of the transfer of value arising and subject to the usual raft of provisions designed to prevent abuse.

It is essential that agricultural activities are being carried out on the land at the time of the transfer.

Farming syndicate arrangements are available to provide Inheritance Tax shelters for investments of £200,000 or more.

7.22 THE SAFETY NET

Given the numerous and highly complex conditions which must be satisfied in order to obtain business property relief or Agricultural Property Relief, the matter will often be in doubt when the business owner dies.

If the owner simply leaves the business or agricultural property to their surviving spouse, the matter will still not be resolved as this transfer will be exempt anyway.

However, if the deceased left the property to a discretionary trust in their Will, Revenue & Customs will need to examine the case and, hopefully, the matter will soon be resolved.

How does this help?

If business property relief or Agricultural Property Relief, as the case may be, is denied, there should be time to enter into a deed of variation (see Section 15.10) amending the Will so that the property is transferred to the surviving spouse free from Inheritance Tax.

The tax is at least deferred and the executors will know where they stand. Furthermore, the surviving spouse may even have time to correct whatever defects there were in the property so that there is a better chance of claiming relief successfully on their subsequent death.

Chapter 8

Miscellaneous Matters

8.1   VALUATIONS

Valuation is a key part of Inheritance Tax. We are frequently concerned with the value of land, buildings, unquoted shares or unincorporated businesses.

Very often, the value of an asset owned by an individual is dependent on the proportion of a larger asset which they own. We saw a very simple example of this with Bjorn's chairs in Section 2.1.

In practice, the most significant examples of this are in the case of unquoted shares. A controlling (i.e. over 50%) shareholding in a private company might be worth £5,000 per share, for example, whilst a small minority holding in the same company might be worth just £600 per share.

These changes in proportionate value can have major implications for any transfers of value which result in the transferor's shareholding falling into a lower value category.

Example

The 10,000 issued shares in Fleetwood Limited are held as follows:

The Peter Green Charitable Trust:	*3,000*
Mick:	*1,000*
John:	*1,500*
Christine:	*500*
Lindsay:	*2,000*
Stevie:	*2,000*

It has been established that shares in the company can be valued as follows:

Holdings of 50% or more: £5,000 per share
Holdings of 25% to 49.9%: £3,000 per share
Holdings of 10% to 24.9%: £2,000 per share
Holdings of less than 10%: £600 per share

Hence, in the absence of any further information, it appears that the shareholdings should be valued as follows:

The Peter Green Charitable Trust: 3,000 x £3,000 = £9m
Mick: 1,000 x £2,000 = £2m
John: 1,500 x £2,000 = £3m
Christine: 500 x £600 = £0.3m
Lindsay: 2,000 x £2,000 = £4m
Stevie: 2,000 x £2,000 = £4m

Mick decides to give one share to his daughter Nikki. This reduces the value of his remaining holding of 999 shares to £599,400 (999 x £600). The gift to Nikki is therefore treated as a transfer of value of £1,400,600 (£2,000,000 - £599,400) despite the fact that her share is worth just £600.

This preposterous result could be absolutely disastrous for Nikki. If Mick should die within three years of making this gift, Nikki could face an Inheritance Tax bill of up to £560,240. All for a share worth just £600!

Let's hope that business property relief is available on these shares and that Nikki does nothing to mess it up. She certainly needs to hope that Fleetwood Limited isn't floated in the next seven years.

With numbers like this, there are clearly times when a gift should not be accepted.

8.2 RELATED PROPERTY

When valuing assets for Inheritance Tax purposes, each person's own assets are usually valued simply on the basis of what they personally own.

However, what we sometimes need to do is to take account of the 'related property' provisions.

In valuing a person's assets for Inheritance Tax purposes, those assets are treated as if they are part of a larger holding of assets made up of all the assets:

- Held by the person themselves,
- Held by their spouse or civil partner, and
- Which have been held by a charity or similar exempt body within the last five years and which were originally transferred to that body by the person, their spouse or civil partner at some time after 15th April 1976.

Let's now return to our previous example to see the effect of these provisions in practice.

Example

Lindsay and Stevie are married. Hence, the shares held by each of them must be valued as part of a hypothetical holding of 4,000 shares.

John and Christine are also married. Furthermore, it turns out that Christine gave the 3,000 shares to the Peter Green Charitable Trust in 1977.

The shares held by John, Christine and the Peter Green Charitable Trust must therefore all be valued as part of a hypothetical holding of 5,000 shares.

The various shareholdings must therefore now be valued as follows for Inheritance Tax purposes:

The Peter Green Charitable Trust: 3,000 x £5,000 = £15m
Mick: 1,000 x £2,000 = £2m
John: 1,500 x £5,000 = £7.5m
Christine: 500 x £5,000 = £2.5m
Lindsay: 2,000 x £3,000 = £6m
Stevie: 2,000 x £3,000 = £6m

Now let us suppose that Christine gives one share to her son Mac. That share, we know, is only worth £600. However, the transfer results in Christine's remaining holding being part of a hypothetical holding of 4,999 shares. This will be worth £3,000 per share, meaning that Christine's remaining 499 shares are deemed to be worth £1,497,000 for Inheritance Tax purposes.

The transfer of value on Christine's gift to Mac is thus £1,003,000 (£2,500,000 - £1,497,000), which is actually more than £700,000 greater than Christine's entire shareholding is worth, not to mention almost 1,700 times the value of Mac's single share.

If Christine should die within three years, Mac could face an Inheritance Tax bill of up to £401,200!

As we can see from this example, the 'related property' provisions can cause further and perhaps unexpected problems with small gifts being given massive hypothetical values for Inheritance Tax purposes.

The most disappointing aspect of this situation is probably the fact that giving assets to charity can result in unexpected Inheritance Tax consequences at any time in the future. There is no seven year time limit here, the impact of the charity's shareholding on your future Inheritance Tax bill is permanent!

8.3   QUICK SUCCESSION RELIEF

Back in the 'bad old days' of estate duty, families were often financially crippled when two generations died in quick succession. Imagine it: just as the family was struggling to recover from one set of death duties, they were landed with another lot. (This happened so much in the First World War that the 'Death on Active Service' exemption, as explained in Section 4.9, was brought in.)

Thankfully, we now have quick succession relief which provides some relief from Inheritance Tax whenever a transferee dies within five years of having received an earlier transfer on which Inheritance Tax was paid, or on which Inheritance Tax subsequently becomes payable (bearing in mind that the tax can arise up to seven years after the original transfer).

Having said that, the value of quick succession relief declines pretty quickly and hence the crippling effects of Inheritance Tax are therefore unfortunately still with us.

The amount of the relief is arrived at by way of the following formula:

QSR = 'Percentage' x Original Tax x Net Transfer/Gross Transfer

The 'Percentage' referred to above is as follows:

Period between original transfer and transferee's death	Percentage
One year or less:	100%
More than one year, but not more than two:	80%
More than two years, but not more than three:	60%
More than three years, but not more than four:	40%
More than four years, but not more than five:	20%

Example

On 5th May 2004, Ewan died and left £600,000 to his daughter Kirsty. The Inheritance Tax on this gift was settled out of Ewan's estate. Grossing-up therefore applied (see Section 2.4), giving rise to an Inheritance Tax bill of £400,000.

Sadly, in December 2006, Kirsty dies in an accident and leaves her estate to her friend Shane.

Kirsty's executors can now claim quick succession relief. The relevant amounts for the calculation are as follows:

Percentage:	*60% (death between two and three years after original transfer)*
Original Tax:	*£400,000*
Net Transfer:	*£600,000*
Gross Transfer:	*£1,000,000 (after applying 'grossing up' on Ewan's death)*

The quick succession relief is therefore:

60% x £400,000 x £600,000/£1,000,000 = £144,000

The reason for the 'Net Transfer/Gross Transfer' element of the formula is to ensure that the relief applies only to the net funds left in the transferee's estate after accounting for the Inheritance Tax payable on the earlier transfer.

If you think about it, Kirsty only received £600,000 from Ewan's estate, so it would be illogical (although nice) for her to get relief for the tax paid on the entire £1m 'grossed-up' gift.

8.4   NATIONAL HERITAGE PROPERTY

Have you ever wondered why so many stately homes are open to the public?

Well, just like the bricked-up windows in old Georgian houses and the roofless buildings we used to see back in the 1970's, it's all because of tax.

Inheritance Tax arising on transfers of 'national heritage property' can be deferred when the owners give an undertaking to conserve and protect the property. They will also need to provide 'reasonable access to the public'.

The conditions to be satisfied in order to claim this exemption are somewhat complex, including, in most cases, the need for the property to be 'pre-eminent for its national, scientific, historic or artistic interest'.

So, simply allowing the punters to look at a couple of rusting chassis in your back garden will probably not qualify.

But, if your uncle leaves you his large collection of classic cars, a claim under the 'national heritage property' provisions might be worth thinking about.

Chapter 9

An Introduction to Trusts

9.1   WHAT IS A TRUST?

In its simplest form, a 'trust' is basically an arrangement under which someone is given the legal title to an asset and is 'trusted' to hold that asset on behalf of one or more beneficiaries.

Some definitions:

'Trustee' - The person trusted to hold the asset.
'Beneficiary' - The person on whose behalf the asset is held.
'Settlor' - The person who transferred the asset into the trust in the first place.

Very often the settlor will also be a trustee. Legally, there is nothing to prevent the settlor from also being a beneficiary, although this usually renders the trust ineffective for Inheritance Tax planning purposes and can also give rise to some unwanted Capital Gains Tax liabilities on the transfers.

Settlements

In legal parlance (and within the tax legislation), the act of putting assets or funds into a trust is generally referred to as a 'settlement'.

Furthermore, every time new assets or funds are put into the trust this represents a new 'settlement'. Each 'settlement' has its own separate identity for Inheritance Tax purposes and this is now especially important in view of the current proposed changes to the taxation position of trusts.

Example

On 20th March 2006, Marc set up the Jeepster Discretionary Trust and transferred £1m into it.

On 25th March 2006, Marc transferred another £1m into the trust.

134

Although there is only one formally constituted trust, Marc has made two settlements, one on 20th March 2006 and one on 25th March 2006.

Assets and funds held within a trust are known as 'Settled Property'. When assets finally leave the trust and become the property of the ultimate beneficiary we say that the beneficiary now holds those assets 'absolutely'.

9.2   WHERE DO WE STAND WITH TRUSTS TODAY?

Trusts have a long and honourable history as a well-established mechanism for protecting the interests of the vulnerable, such as orphans or disabled people.

This is not how the Government sees them, however, as is quite apparent from the current attack which is taking final shape in Parliament as I write this edition of *How to Avoid Inheritance Tax*.

Our current Government seems to think that trusts are used almost exclusively to avoid tax!

(OK, I must admit that trusts are very useful for avoiding Inheritance Tax. After all, that's why we've got this chapter in the guide, isn't it?)

The Chancellor of the Exchequer's Budget statement on 22nd March 2006 included proposals for some fundamental changes to the way in which trusts are treated for Inheritance Tax purposes.

At the time of writing, these proposed changes are still being debated in Parliament and the relevant legislation is unlikely to be finalised for several more weeks. Even then, it may take some time before we see how Revenue & Customs intend to interpret the new rules.

In compiling this edition of this guide, I have attempted to analyse the effect of the proposed changes on the Inheritance Tax planning techniques discussed. Readers must be aware, however, that the proposed changes to the Inheritance Tax legislation are not yet final, so my analysis is therefore somewhat provisional at this stage.

Before we move on to some of those useful Inheritance Tax planning techniques, however, we need to understand a bit more about trusts, how they are treated for tax purposes and how they will be treated in the future.

As we are currently in a 'state of transition' with trusts, we will need to look at both the 'old rules' applying before 22nd March 2006 and the 'new rules' which have been proposed and which will apply to new settlements from 22nd March 2006 onwards.

9.3   WHAT TYPES OF TRUST ARE THERE?

There are many different types of trust, including the following:

- Bare Trusts
- Interest In Possession Trusts
- Life Interest Trusts
- Discretionary Trusts
- Accumulation and Maintenance Trusts
- A Trust For A Bereaved Minor
- Disabled Trusts
- Charitable Trusts

However, in essence, there are only really two kinds of trust, an 'interest in possession trust' and a 'discretionary trust'. Why then did I bother listing eight different categories of trust? I did this because all of the other categories, whilst simply being specialised sub-groups of the two main kinds of trust, have different treatments for Inheritance Tax purposes.

Bare trusts and life interest trusts are basically just types of interest in possession trusts, whilst accumulation and maintenance trusts, disabled trusts and charitable trusts are specialised forms of discretionary trusts. A trust for a bereaved minor is a new concept introduced on 22nd March 2006 and might be either discretionary or involve an interest in possession.

A single trust may hold some assets which are held in a discretionary trust and others which are held in an interest in possession trust, so we can also get a sort of 'hybrid' trust which will be subject to different rules on its different parts.

9.4   INTEREST IN POSSESSION TRUSTS

An interest in possession trust is one where a specific individual is beneficially entitled to all income from, or to otherwise enjoy, the assets of the trust for a specified period. The person entitled to the income from, or enjoyment of, the trust assets has an 'interest in possession'.

Where more than one person is to share the income or enjoyment of the assets for a specified period, this is also an interest in possession trust.

In such cases, the income may be shared in any proportion specified in the Trust Deed.

If, however, the trustees have discretion over the income paid to the beneficiaries, this would make the trust a discretionary trust (see Section 9.9 below).

Example

Nicole transfers a number of investment properties into the All Saints Trust. Under the terms of the trust, each year's rental profits must be paid to the beneficiaries as follows:

- *Half to Nicole's sister, Natalie*

- *The first £10,000 of the remainder to her friend, Melanie,*

- *The remaining balance to her niece, Shaznay*

Each beneficiary's interest is an interest in possession because each of them receives a specific defined amount under the terms of the Trust Deed which is not dependent on the discretion of the trustees.

The Remainder

'The remainder' is a term which is often used to describe the right to assets which comes into force after an interest in possession ends. The most common example would be when a person leaves a life interest in property to their spouse with the remainder to their children. This would mean that, on the spouse's death, the property passes absolutely to the children.

Reversion to Settlor

It is worth noting that it is possible to create an interest in possession trust where the remainder interest reverts to the original settlor. This, in itself, does not invoke the 'Gift with Reservation' rules (see Section 5.9), as long as the settlor and the spouse are excluded from any benefit during the period that the interest in possession exists.

9.5   LIFE INTEREST TRUSTS

A life interest is simply an interest in possession where the specified period of the beneficiary's interest is the remainder of their life.

Generally speaking, therefore, the Inheritance Tax treatment of a life interest trust is exactly the same as any other interest in possession trust.

9.6   BARE TRUSTS

Minors under the age of 18 cannot take legal title to property in England or Wales.

The position in Scotland is slightly different and legal title is sometimes possible at 16.

Assets which are simply held in someone else's name (i.e. an adult) on behalf of a minor are held on 'bare trust'. A bare trust is sometimes also known as an 'absolute trust'.

A bare trust only exists where the minor has full beneficial ownership of the trust assets, both in terms of capital and income, and the minor will become absolutely entitled to the asset on reaching the age of 18 (sometimes 16 in Scotland). The trust may, however, continue beyond this point until such time as the beneficiary calls for the trust assets to be transferred to them.

Assets held on bare trust are simply treated as belonging to the beneficiary for Inheritance Tax purposes. Furthermore, the treatment of bare trusts is unaffected by the current proposed changes. We will see some useful consequences of this in the next chapter.

9.7   INHERITANCE TAX TREATMENT OF OLD INTEREST IN POSSESSION TRUSTS

Under the old rules prior to 22nd March 2006, whenever a beneficiary had an interest in possession they were treated, for Inheritance Tax purposes, as if they owned the asset outright.

Subject to certain exceptions, the termination of their interest, whether on death or otherwise, therefore represented the transfer of the underlying asset for Inheritance Tax purposes.

This treatment still continues to apply to all interests in possession which existed in settlements made before 22nd March 2006.

Wealth Warning

Note that the old rules may only apply to **'settlements'** made before 22nd March 2006. Any new transfer of assets into an existing trust will constitute a new settlement and, at present, it is not clear how such transferred assets will be treated.

Furthermore, where an interest in possession in a settlement made before 22nd March 2006 comes to an end before 6th April 2008 and is replaced by a new interest in possession within the same trust, the old rules also continue to apply to that new interest in possession.

Example

Maurice died on 10th December 2005 and left a life interest in all of his assets to his brother Barry. Under the terms of Maurice's Will, on Barry's death, the assets are to remain in trust for the benefit of Maurice's nephew, Robin.

If Barry dies before 6th April 2008, the old rules will continue to apply to Robin's interest in possession.

Old Interests In Possession Coming to an End - Summary

To summarise, the Inheritance Tax consequences on the termination of an interest in possession which is subject to the old rules are as follows:

Interest in possession ends on death of beneficiary before 6th April 2008	**Assets included in beneficiary's estate for Inheritance Tax purposes. Any new interest in possession coming into existence is also subject to <u>old</u> rules.**
Interest in possession ends during beneficiary's lifetime but before 6th April 2008	**Usually a potentially exempt transfer if assets pass absolutely or a new interest in possession comes into existence. Any new interest in possession coming into existence is also subject to <u>old</u> rules.**
Interest in possession ends on death of beneficiary on or after 6th April 2008	**Assets included in beneficiary's estate for Inheritance Tax purposes. Any new interest in possession coming into existence is subject to <u>new</u> rules.**
Interest in possession ends during beneficiary's lifetime on or after 6th April 2008	**Only a potentially exempt transfer if assets pass absolutely. If assets remain in trust there is a chargeable lifetime transfer. Any new interest in possession coming into existence is subject to <u>new</u> rules.**

Reversion To Settlor

One of the most important exceptions to the general rules applying to pre-22nd March 2006 settlements is that, when property reverts to the original settlor on the termination of an interest in possession, the resultant transfer of value is exempt from Inheritance Tax. We will see how this exception has been put to good use later, in Chapter 13.

9.8 INHERITANCE TAX TREATMENT OF NEW INTEREST IN POSSESSION TRUSTS

Subject to a few exceptions which we will examine later in this chapter, any new settlement made on or after 22nd March 2006 by way of a lifetime transfer will be regarded as 'relevant property'. Broadly, this means that the same rules which apply to discretionary trusts will apply to that settlement regardless of whether an interest in possession exists or not.

These rules are set out in detail in Sections 9.14 to 9.17. In essence, Inheritance Tax arises when the settlement is made, when assets come out of the trust, and every ten years whilst they're in it.

Remember, as explained previously, this may apply to any new lifetime settlement, not just a newly constituted trust. This is of particular concern when we consider life policies held in trust and we will return to this in Section 11.9.

Transfers on Death

From 22nd March 2006, any new interests in possession created on death will also be subject to the 'relevant property' regime, as explained in Sections 9.14 to 9.17, except for:

- Interests in possession held by surviving spouses, and
- Qualifying 'immediate post-death interests' (see below)

Surviving Spouses

One piece of good news is that, under the latest proposals, it now appears that any interest in possession arising on death which is held by the deceased's surviving spouse should generally be exempt from the 'relevant property' regime. The assets subject to the interest in possession should therefore be treated as part of the surviving spouse's estate until their interest in possession comes to an end (usually on their death in most cases).

When the surviving spouse's interest comes to an end, this will be treated as a 'transfer of value' of the underlying assets held in the trust. If this transfer takes place on the spouse's death, the underlying assets will be treated as part of their estate.

If the spouse's interest ends during their lifetime, the resultant 'transfer of value' will be a potentially exempt transfer if another person becomes absolutely entitled to the trust assets or they pass to a disabled trust. In most other cases a chargeable lifetime transfer arises.

If the assets remain in trust after the spouse's interest comes to an end, they will be treated as 'relevant property' (see Section 9.14) from that time onwards, unless they fall within one of exceptions (ii), (iii) or (iv) below.

Immediate Post-Death Interest

Subject to the general exemption for interests in possession held by surviving spouses, any other new interests in possession created on death will be treated as 'relevant property' unless, on the termination of that interest in possession,

> i) Another individual becomes absolutely entitled to the property,
> ii) A 'trust for a bereaved minor' (see Section 9.11) comes into existence,
> iii) A disabled trust comes into existence, or
> iv) The property passes to charity.

Unless the interest in possession arising on death is held by the deceased's spouse, the new rules require that one of the above four transfers **must** take place on the termination of the 'immediate post-death interest' (i.e. the interest in possession coming into existence on the deceased's death). If there is *any possibility* that anything else might occur, the interest in possession trust arising on death will then be 'relevant property'.

Furthermore, to avoid 'relevant property' treatment, any power of the trustees to terminate the original 'immediate post-death interest' must be limited to either:

i) A power which can only be applied to benefit the interest in possession beneficiary, or
ii) A power which can only be exercised by or with the consent of the interest in possession beneficiary.

Broadly then, what kinds of legacies left in trust can avoid being treated as 'relevant property'?

New Qualifying Trusts

The following types of interest in possession created on the transferor's death are **examples** of interests in possession which will still qualify for the old rules and will therefore not be treated as 'relevant property':

- Any life interest (or other interest in possession) for the deceased's surviving spouse.
- A life interest for the deceased's unmarried common-law partner with the remainder to the deceased's children.
- A life interest for the deceased's unmarried common-law partner which will be followed by a 'trust for a bereaved minor' in the event of the partner's death before the deceased's children reach the age of 18.
- An interest in possession for the deceased's brother which is followed by a disabled trust for the benefit of the deceased's mentally handicapped nephew when the nephew reaches the age of 25.
- A life interest for the deceased's daughter after which the assets are to be left to charity.

The interest in possession created on death under the above settlements will be treated as part of the estate of the beneficiary. If that interest in possession comes to an end on the beneficiary's death, the assets of the trust will be treated as part of the beneficiary's estate.

If the 'immediate post-death interest' ends during the beneficiary's lifetime, the resultant transfer of the assets of the trust will be regarded as a lifetime transfer by that beneficiary. In most cases, that transfer would be a potentially exempt transfer.

Non-Qualifying Trusts

At present, the following types of interest in possession created on the transferor's death would not appear to qualify to be treated under the old rules and would therefore be 'relevant property':

- A life interest for a surviving unmarried common-law partner followed by a life interest for the deceased's children.
- A life interest for a surviving unmarried common-law partner with remainder to the deceased's children unless any of those children pre-decease the surviving partner in which case that child's share is to be held on trust for the benefit of the deceased's grandchildren.
- An interest in possession for a surviving unmarried common-law partner which terminates in the event of his or her marriage.
- A life interest for a surviving unmarried common-law partner to be followed by an interest in possession trust for the deceased's children in the event that the surviving partner dies before the youngest child reaches the age of 25.

These examples may seem like perfectly sensible arrangements but each would result in the unmarried common-law partner's life interest being treated as 'relevant property' and therefore subject to the anniversary and exit charges outlined in Sections 9.15 and 9.16. This may not be all bad, however, as at least the assets held in the trust would not be exposed to an Inheritance Tax charge on the common-law partner's death.

9.9   DISCRETIONARY TRUSTS

A discretionary trust is basically any trust, or part thereof, where no person is entitled to an interest in possession. The trustees therefore have the discretion to decide who to allow to have the enjoyment of the trust's assets, who to pay the income of the trust to and how much.

There is usually a defined class of beneficiaries from whom the trustees can choose, such as "all my grandchildren", for example. The assets of a discretionary trust will be treated as 'relevant property' (see Section 9.14) unless the trust qualifies as:

- An accumulation and maintenance trust (Section 9.10),
- A 'trust for a bereaved minor' (Section 9.11),
- A disabled trust (Section 9.12), or
- A charitable trust (Section 4.8).

9.10 ACCUMULATION AND MAINTENANCE TRUSTS

The Good Old Days

Before 22nd March 2006, the assets within an accumulation and maintenance trust enjoyed a near-complete exemption from Inheritance Tax. Transfers into the trust were treated as potentially exempt transfers, assets within the trust were exempt from Inheritance Tax and there were no charges on the death of a beneficiary or a transfer of assets out of the trust. The qualifying conditions for accumulation and maintenance trusts set up before 22nd March 2006 were as follows:

i) One or more of the trust beneficiaries will become entitled to the trust assets, or to a life interest therein, on attaining a specified age, not exceeding 25.

ii) There is no 'interest in possession' in any of the trust assets.

iii) Income from trust assets is to be accumulated within the trust unless applied for the maintenance, education or general benefit of the beneficiaries.

iv) Either:
    a. No more than 25 years have elapsed since the trust was established or, if later, first satisfied conditions (i) to (iii), or
    b. All beneficiaries, past and present, either share a common grandparent or are children, widows or widowers of such persons who died before they would have become entitled as under condition (i) above.

A Rude Awakening

From 22nd March 2006, any new accumulation and maintenance trusts set up by way of a lifetime transfer will be subject to the 'relevant property' rules (see Sections 9.14 to 9.17) unless they qualify as a disabled trust.

Existing accumulation and maintenance trusts will be able to keep their privileged status but only if the terms of the trust are amended in line with the new rules for a 'trust for a bereaved minor'. These rules are set out in Section 9.11 below, although conditions (ii) and (iii) do not apply in these circumstances. Existing accumulation and maintenance trusts may alternatively retain partial exemption, as explained in Section 9.11, if the terms of the trust are amended, but with any age not in excess of 25 substituted in place of 18.

Trustees of existing accumulation and maintenance trusts have until 5th April 2008 to make the appropriate amendments to the terms of the trust in order to keep the trust's exempt status, or at least retain partial exemption. In practice, for many accumulation and maintenance trusts, this will simply not be possible.

9.11   TRUST FOR A BEREAVED MINOR

Under the current proposals, the privileges previously afforded to accumulation and maintenance trusts will be 'inherited' (pardon the pun!) by a new, much more restrictive class of trust, the 'trust for a bereaved minor'. The assets will be exempt from Inheritance Tax and there will be no charges if a beneficiary dies or assets are transferred out of the trust. The basic conditions are:

i)   The beneficiary of the trust must be under 18 years of age.
ii)   At least one of the beneficiary's parents is dead.
iii) Trust was set up under a) Intestacy b) the criminal injuries compensation scheme or c) the will of a deceased parent.
iv) Beneficiary absolutely entitled to trust assets at age 18.
v)   Trust assets may only be applied for the benefit of the minor until he or she reaches the age of 18.
vi) Trust income may either be applied for the benefit of the minor or given directly to them.

One relaxation from the previous trust rules is that the minor may have an interest in possession, if the settlor so desires. The major problem with the proposed new rules, however, is that the beneficiary must gain absolute possession of the trust assets at the age of 18. Many people are horrified at the prospect of the entire family fortune suddenly being at the whim of someone so young. The chances of them frittering everything away before they have the wisdom to look out for their own future are all too obvious.

Partial Exemption

Thankfully, in order to meet these concerns, it is now proposed that a trust for a bereaved minor will retain a form of partial exemption when the above rules are met except for the fact that an age not exceeding 25 is substituted in place of 18 in conditions (iv) and (v).

Where this partial exemption applies, the trust assets will only become 'relevant property' when the beneficiary reaches the age of 18 (rather than on the settlor's death, as originally proposed). There will be no Inheritance Tax charge when the trust assets become 'relevant property' on the beneficiary's 18th birthday, but the exit charges explained in Section 9.16 will then apply as if the trust had been set up on this date. This means that there will be a maximum exit charge of 4.2% if the trust assets pass to the beneficiary at the age of 25. (In addition to the Inheritance Tax already paid on the parent's death.)

Multiple Beneficiaries

The above rules are clearly designed for a single beneficiary. It would appear, however, that a trust may still qualify with two or more beneficiaries as long as each of them obtains absolute entitlement to their own share of the trust assets at the age of 18 (or by the age of 25 in the case of 'partial exemption').

9.12 DISABLED TRUSTS

Assets within a qualifying disabled trust are exempt from the 'relevant property' provisions and are instead treated as being part of the beneficiary's estate. The qualifying conditions are as follows:

i) During the life of a disabled person there is no 'interest in possession' in any of the trust assets. (Ironically, however, these trusts are the only trusts to still enjoy the treatment given to old-style interest in possession trusts!)

ii) Not less than half of the funds applied by the trust during the disabled person's lifetime are applied for the benefit of that disabled person.

iii) The 'disabled person' is:
   a. incapable of managing their own affairs by reason of a mental disorder in terms of the Mental Health Act,
   b. in receipt of an attendance allowance, or
   c. in receipt of a disability living allowance with a care component at the higher or middle rate.

9.13   SUMMARY SO FAR

Before 22nd March 2006, only discretionary trusts were subject to the 'relevant property' regime which we will examine in Sections 9.14 to 9.17. For this reason, that regime is sometimes referred to as 'the discretionary trust regime'. This name no longer seems appropriate however. Under the current proposals, from 22nd March 2006, all trusts will be subject to the 'relevant property' regime except:

- Bare trusts
- Disabled trusts
- Charitable trusts
- Interest in possession trusts for a surviving spouse
- Immediate post-death interest trusts
- A trust for a bereaved minor
- Pre- 22nd March 2006 interest in possession trusts (until an interest in possession ends after 5th April 2008)
- Pre- 22nd March 2006 accumulation and maintenance trusts which successfully convert to a trust for a bereaved minor

9.14   THE RELEVANT PROPERTY REGIME

To make life easier, let's refer to any trust which falls into the relevant property regime as a 'relevant property trust'. A relevant property trust is treated as being a separate and distinct person in its own right for Inheritance Tax purposes.

This has the following major consequences:

- Lifetime transfers into a relevant property trust are chargeable transfers not potentially exempt transfers.

- Transfers into a relevant property trust on death will generally be ineligible for the spouse exemption.

- Assets within a relevant property trust are not generally included in a beneficiary's estate for Inheritance Tax purposes.

- No charges arise on the death of a beneficiary or termination of their interest in the trust's assets, but

- A charge may arise when assets leave the trust (see Section 9.16),

- There is no 'revert to settlor' exemption (see Section 9.7),

- Ten-year anniversary charges apply (see Section 9.15)

In essence, therefore, Inheritance Tax arises when assets go into a relevant property trust, when they come out of it, and every ten years whilst they're in it.

Nevertheless, a relevant property trust's 'separate life' does give rise to some very useful tax-planning opportunities, which we will consider further later, in Chapters 10 and 13.

9.15   TEN-YEAR ANNIVERSARY CHARGES

Unfortunately, to counter the possible advantages of a relevant property trust's 'separate life', these trusts are subject to an Inheritance Tax charge on every tenth anniversary of their creation.

We will now examine how this charge is calculated.

It gets complex but all will become clear when we work through a practical example at the end.

The anniversary charge is calculated as follows:

i) The value of all relevant property in the trust on the anniversary date must be calculated.

ii) Add any other property in the trust on the day that it was transferred into the trust or, if later, the date that it ceased to be relevant property.

iii) Add any non-charitable settlements made into other trusts by the same settlor on the same day.

iv) The amount of Inheritance Tax payable on a chargeable lifetime transfer of the total of (i) to (iii) on the Anniversary Date is calculated taking account of:
    a. The nil rate band, but not any other exemptions, and
    b. Any actual chargeable transfers made by the Settlor in the seven years prior to making the settlement into this trust (adjusted, as appropriate, for any Potentially Exempt Transfers which became chargeable if that settlor has died since setting up the trust).

v) Using the amount derived at step (iv), the 'Effective Rate' of Inheritance Tax on the hypothetical lifetime transfer is calculated.

vi) The 'Effective Rate' is multiplied by 3/10ths and applied to any amounts in (i) above derived from assets which have been held by the trust throughout the ten-year period.

vii) For any amounts within (i) which are derived from assets held for less than ten years, the charge is reduced by one fortieth for every complete calendar quarter that those assets were not held as relevant assets of the Trust.

viii) The rate applying to any charges under (vii) above may, however, be increased to take account of further chargeable transfers made by the settlor since setting up the trust (other than those actually made to the trust itself). (E.g. where the settlor made a potentially exempt transfer the year after setting up the trust which has become chargeable due to their death within seven years.)

Now _that_ calls for an example!

As usual, all exemptions and reliefs other than the nil rate band will be ignored, for the sake of simplicity.

Example

On 1st April 1997, Mel set up the Spice Discretionary Trust for the benefit of her granddaughters, Emma and Melanie, and any further issue of her children (i.e. any more grandchildren she might have).

She transferred various assets into the trust at that date. The total value of the assets transferred at that time was £80,000, and hence no Inheritance Tax was payable on Mel's chargeable lifetime transfer because the amount was below the nil rate band.

On the same day, she also transferred £50,000 into an old-style interest in possession trust for her niece Victoria.

Previously, on 22nd November 1996, Mel had also given her sister Geri £110,000.

Sadly, Mel passed away in January 2003. (Fortunately, the nil rate band was available to cover all of her lifetime transfers within the previous seven years, which all became chargeable at this time.)

On 1st April 2007, the assets in the Spice Discretionary Trust are worth £300,000.

The anniversary charge is calculated as follows:

	£
Value of relevant property on anniversary date:	300,000
Other settlement made on the same day:	50,000
Previous chargeable transfers:	110,000
(i.e. the Potentially Exempt Transfer to Geri, which became chargeable on Mel's death in 2003)	
Cumulative total for hypothetical transfer:	**460,000**
Less nil rate band	285,000
Gives:	175,000

| *Inheritance Tax at lifetime rate (20%)* | ***35,000*** |

'Effective Rate' of Inheritance Tax on the
hypothetical transfer:
(£35,000 divided by £300,000 PLUS £50,000,
expressed as a percentage)   *10%*

Rate for anniversary charge:
3/10ths of 10%   *3%*

Inheritance Tax Payable:
3% x £300,000   ***9,000***

The result of this rather tortuous calculation is that Inheritance Tax of only £9,000 is payable on the assets in the Spice Discretionary Trust.

Remember that, had these assets still been in Mel's estate at the time of her death, Inheritance Tax of up to £120,000 would have been payable on them.

Tax Tip

The position would have been better if Geri had waited until the next day to make the gift into Victoria's interest in possession trust.

In fact, the ten year anniversary charge would then have been just £7,500.

It may be better, therefore, to delay other settlements until the day after any chargeable transfer into a relevant property trust.

Having said that, however, most settlements after 21st March 2006 will be chargeable transfers now anyway and the interests of both sets of beneficiaries will need to be taken into account.

Undistributed Versus Accumulated Income

Trust income which has simply not yet been distributed to beneficiaries at the date of the anniversary is not included in 'relevant property' for the purposes of the ten year anniversary charge. (Nor for any 'exit charges' – see Section 9.16 below.)

However, once the trustees have 'accumulated' that income, it does become part of the relevant property of the trust. Broadly, it is then treated like a new transfer of value made on the date of the 'accumulation'.

Income is 'accumulated' when the trustees decide not to distribute it to the trust's beneficiaries. Generally speaking, income will be accumulated if it has still not been distributed at the end of the relevant tax year.

The exact date of 'accumulation' is somewhat difficult to determine but will generally be sometime between the date of receipt and the end of the relevant tax year.

9.16   EXIT CHARGES

Transfers of assets out of a relevant property trust may also give rise to Inheritance Tax charges.

These 'Exit Charges' are broadly based on similar principles to the ten-year Anniversary Charge. The 'Effective Rate' (see example in Section 9.15 above) arrived at in each case is multiplied by three tenths, and then also multiplied by one fortieth for every complete calendar quarter expiring since the most recent ten-year Anniversary, or since the creation of the trust in the case of transfers taking place within the first ten years.

For an Exit Charge arising in the first ten-year period, the Hypothetical Lifetime Transfer used to derive the Effective Rate is based on the value of the assets in the trust at its commencement, plus any further settlements made into the trust between then and the date of the transfer.

Example

Let's assume the same facts as in the example in Section 9.15 above, except that:

    i)   *On 25th December 2002, Mel transferred a further £10,000 into the Spice Discretionary Trust, and*

    ii) *On 30th June 2006, the trustees give £20,000 to Emma out of capital.*

The exit charge on Emma's gift is calculated as follows:

	£
Value of property settled on 1st April 1997:	*80,000*
Other settlement made on the same day:	*50,000*
Previous chargeable transfers:	*110,000*
Value of property settled on 25th December 2002:	*10,000*
Cumulative total for hypothetical transfer:	***250,000***
nil rate band	*285,000*
Therefore, Inheritance Tax Payable:	***NIL***

Tax Tip

As this example so ably demonstrates, Inheritance Tax can often be avoided when the trust's assets are distributed to beneficiaries before the first ten year anniversary of the trust. We will look at the opportunities which this provides in more detail in Chapter 10.

To finish our look at exit charges, however, let's make a slight revision to our example.

Example Revised

Let's now assume that the gift to Geri which became chargeable on Mel's death was actually £210,000.

What does this do to Emma's exit charge?

The cumulative total for the hypothetical transfer is now £350,000.

Deducting the nil rate band of £285,000, leaves:	*£65,000*
Inheritance Tax at lifetime rate (20%)	*£13,000*

*'Effective Rate' of Inheritance Tax on the
hypothetical transfer:*
(£13,000 divided by £140,000*)   *9.286%*
(* - £80,000 + £50,000 + £10,000)

Rate for anniversary charge:
9.286% x 3/10 x 36/40   *2.507%*

Inheritance Tax Payable:
2.507% x £20,000   ***£501***

Points To Note

i) If Emma bears the tax, the exit charge will be £501, as above. However, if the trust were to bear the tax 'grossing up' would apply. The 'grossing up' rate in this case would be 2.507/97.493, giving rise to a 'grossed up' charge, at 2.571%, of £514.

ii) Only 36 and not 37 calendar quarters are counted here. The 37th quarter does not end until 30th June 2006 and, as the transfer to Emma took place on that date, this quarter had not yet expired. If the transfer had been made one day later, we would have needed to include the 37th quarter.

Later Exit Charges are based on the Effective Rate applying at the last previous ten-year Anniversary, as adjusted for any further settlements into the trust since then.

Distributions of income out of the trust do not give rise to Exit Charges. Care must be taken, however, that the income is not allowed to 'accumulate' first before distribution.

9.17 DEATH OF SETTLOR

As we know, when the settlor dies, all of the potentially exempt transfers which they made within the last seven years of their life become chargeable transfers.

This may lead to retrospective increases to the amount of any exit charges or ten year anniversary charges where the settlor has also made transfers of value into a relevant property trust within that same seven year period.

Chapter 10

Inheritance Tax Planning With Trusts

10.1   USING RELEVANT PROPERTY TRUSTS

Because relevant property trusts are effectively treated as separate persons for Inheritance Tax purposes, they provide an opportunity to shelter assets in a vehicle which exists outside of any individual person's estate. (Subject, of course, to the anniversary and exit charges explained in Chapter 9.)

In theory, the planning techniques using discretionary trusts outlined in this chapter should now apply equally to all relevant property trusts, so that a new interest in possession trust created on or after 22nd March 2006 will do just as well as a discretionary trust.

However, as the current proposed changes have not yet been finalised, my advice, for the time being at least, is to continue to use a discretionary trust for any Inheritance Tax planning technique which required a discretionary trust prior to 22nd March 2006.

10.2   THE DISCRETIONARY TRUST SHELTER

In effect, and subject to any other transfers which you may be making, there is the opportunity to transfer assets equal in value to the nil rate band into discretionary trusts every seven years free from Inheritance Tax.

In fact, taking the annual exemption, and the fact that the nil rate band generally increases every year, into account, it will be possible to accumulate a considerable amount of value within the discretionary trust.

Please note that there are some drawbacks to this method, which we will look at in Section 10.8.

Leaving those to one side for the moment though, let's look at an example with a wealthy couple starting their Inheritance Tax planning this year.

Example

Salvatore and Cherilyn are a wealthy married couple with adult children. Neither of them has made any transfer of value prior to 6th April 2006. On that date they set up the Caesar & Cleo Discretionary Trust with their children as the beneficiaries and each transfer £291,000 into it. The first £6,000 of each person's transfer is covered by their annual exemptions and the remaining £285,000 by their nil rate band. Hence, whilst there is a chargeable lifetime transfer, no Inheritance Tax is payable at this stage. A total of £582,000 is now 'sheltered' in the trust.

On 6th April 2007, Salvatore and Cherilyn are each able to put a further £18,000 into the trust. £3,000 of each transfer is covered by the annual exemption, leaving a chargeable lifetime transfer of £15,000. This brings each person's cumulative chargeable transfers up to £300,000 (£285,000 plus £15,000), which is covered by the nil rate band for 2007/2008. A total of £618,000 has now been transferred to the trust free from Inheritance Tax.

The couple then follow the same principles for another five years, as follows:

Date	*Transfer (Each)*	*Total Value Transferred To Date (Both)*
6th April 2008	*£15,000*	*£648,000*
6th April 2009	*£16,000*	*£680,000*
6th April 2010	*£13,000*	*£706,000*
6th April 2011	*£14,000*	*£734,000*
6th April 2012	*£14,000*	*£762,000*

(Based on the nil rate bands which we already know up to 2009/2010 and then on the assumption that it increases at the rate of 3% per annum thereafter.)

After 6th April 2013, however, the first transfers made by the couple on 6th April 2006 will no longer need to be counted when calculating their cumulative chargeable transfers.

On 7th April 2013, Salvatore and Cherilyn will therefore each be able to transfer £299,000 into the Caesar & Cleo Discretionary Trust free from Inheritance Tax. This is because, at this point, each person's cumulative chargeable lifetime transfers in the last seven years are just £72,000. The projected nil rate band at this point (following the principles explained above) is £368,000, meaning that each of them can make a new chargeable transfer of £296,000 without giving rise to any Inheritance Tax. Adding the annual exemption gives a total tax-free transfer of £299,000 each. These latest transfers bring the total value transferred into the trust to date up to £1,360,000.

Following the same principles for the next two years produces the following results:

Date	Transfer (Each)	Total Value Transferred To Date (Both)
7th April 2014	£30,000	£1,420,000
7th April 2015	£27,000	£1,474,000

Great – almost £1.5m has now been 'sheltered'. However, on 6th April 2016, our 'shelter' springs a bit of a leak – the ten-year anniversary charge hits.

To calculate this charge, let's assume that all of the trust's income has been distributed to the beneficiaries each year, but that the assets within the trust have grown in value at the rate of 10% per annum (compound).

This produces a total value for the trust assets at 6th April 2016 of £2,781,200.

The next important point to note is that the transfers made by each of the two settlors will be treated separately, so that each has their own nil rate band (which is now £404,000 per our projections).

The calculation of the ten year anniversary charge is quite complex, but basically, the 'Effective Rate' is derived by taking 20% of the value of trust assets in excess of two nil rate bands as a percentage of the value of those assets. In this case, the 'Effective Rate' is 14.19% (£2,781,200 – 2 x £404,000 = £1,973,200 x 20% = £394,640, which, divided by £2,781,200, produces a rate of 14.19%).

This rate is then multiplied by 3/10ths and then one fortieth of this result is deducted for each calendar quarter that the relevant assets were not in the trust.

The assets in the trust from the outset are therefore subject to a charge of 4.26%. The assets which have been in the trust for nine years suffer a charge of 3.83%, those held for eight years suffer 3.41%, and so on.

In total, the anniversary charge amounts to just £85,430.

This may seem like a lot of money, but it represents just 3% of the value of the assets in the trust. If Salvatore and Cherilyn still held those assets personally, they would be exposed to potential Inheritance Tax charges of 40%, or £1,112,480. The potential saving is therefore huge.

10.3   SERIAL TRUSTS

There is one major drawback to the method used by Salvatore and Cherilyn in the previous section. By using just one trust, they had access to just one extra nil rate band each.

It would actually be better to set up a new trust every seven years and thus continually increase the number of nil rate bands available.

Hence, what Salvatore and Cherilyn should have done is to set up the Caesar and Cleo No. 2 Discretionary Trust on 7th April 2013 and make their next seven years' worth of transfers into that trust. Then, on 8th April 2020, they could set up the Caesar and Cleo No. 3 Discretionary Trust, and so on, for as long as they are able.

For a start, this more sophisticated approach would have reduced the charge arising on 6th April 2016 to £59,141.

The longer-term calculations for this planning technique get quite horrendous but, if Salvatore and Cherilyn are lucky enough to last until 8th April 2026, then, on the basis of our projection methodology set out in Section 10.2 above, they would then have the following assets in trust:

Caesar and Cleo Discretionary Trust:	£4,440,154
Caesar and Cleo No. 2 Discretionary Trust:	£2,800,026
Caesar and Cleo No. 3 Discretionary Trust:	£1,770,412
Total:	£9,010,592

The above figures take account of anniversary charges of £59,141 in 2016, £71,866 in 2023 and £213,329 in 2026. The total Inheritance Tax paid so far is thus £344,336.

This compares with the potential Inheritance Tax of £3,604,237 had these assets still been held by Salvatore and Cherilyn personally.

10.4 HOW USEFUL IS THE DISCRETIONARY TRUST SHELTER?

The first point to note is that you don't need to be in a couple to use this technique. It works just as well for an individual; you just have to halve all the numbers.

Secondly, however, it must be admitted that there are some restrictions to this technique and we will examine these in Section 10.8.

You may also wonder whether using discretionary trusts to shelter assets is really effective in view of the anniversary and exit charges.

It is worth bearing in mind, however, that the tenth anniversary charges arising under the method given in Section 10.3 generally only work out at around 3.5%. Twentieth anniversary charges (if the assets are still in trust at that time) will tend to be higher, say around 4.5% and, if you get to a thirtieth anniversary, we can expect charges of over 5%.

In general, however, the anniversary charges within the trusts are likely to work out at less than 0.5% per annum on average. This effectively means that you would need to live another 80 years after setting up the trust before the anniversary charges began to exceed the tax saved on your death.

Following the serial trust method set out in Section 10.3, I have been able to calculate the projected Inheritance Tax savings for a couple based on the number of years they survive after starting the plan. These are set out below.

Years Survived	Total Net Assets In Trust	Total Net Assets In Estate	Saving
1	£675,767	£645,720	£30,047
2	£772,138	£713,892	£58,246
3	£879,330	£789,921	£89,409
4	£990,312	£866,513	£123,799
5	£1,113,439	£951,965	£161,474
6	£1,247,824	£1,045,081	£202,743
7	£1,965,059	£1,488,629	£476,429
8	£2,214,461	£1,653,652	£560,809
9	£2,480,609	£1,830,617	£649,992
10	£2,773,000	£2,025,519	£747,481
11	£3,091,780	£2,237,351	£854,429
12	£3,441,867	£2,470,526	£971,340
13	£3,824,155	£2,725,979	£1,098,177
14	£4,814,605	£3,349,937	£1,464,668
15	£5,362,384	£3,712,370	£1,650,014
16	£5,956,511	£4,108,327	£1,848,184
17	£6,607,087	£4,543,880	£2,063,207
18	£7,318,997	£5,021,388	£2,297,609
19	£8,098,418	£5,546,567	£2,551,851
20	£8,949,538	£6,122,983	£2,826,555
21	£10,460,329	£7,100,962	£3,359,367
22	£11,576,720	£7,852,578	£3,724,142
23	£12,794,060	£8,677,596	£4,116,464
24	£14,127,727	£9,586,875	£4,540,851
25	£15,585,803	£10,584,363	£5,001,440
26	£17,182,561	£11,683,279	£5,499,281
27	£18,926,534	£12,890,487	£6,036,046
28	£21,415,508	£14,563,216	£6,852,292
29	£23,600,495	£16,078,737	£7,521,757
30	£25,987,089	£17,744,931	£8,242,158

Notes

i) In compiling the above figures, it is assumed that the trusts are wound up at the time of the couple's death. This does not necessarily need to happen, but I have done so here in order to make the comparison fair. The 'Total Net Assets In Trust' are the remaining funds distributed to beneficiaries after dealing with all Inheritance Tax charges suffered at this time. 'Grossing Up' has been applied to the final exit charges.

ii) 'Total Net Assets In Estate' is the total net sum left in the estate after Inheritance Tax from the same assets if these had been retained personally. To create a fair 'like with like' comparison, it is assumed that the deceased's nil rate band is used against these assets.

iii) 'Saving' is, broadly speaking, the overall net tax saving. To be more accurate though, it is actually the additional amount left to the beneficiaries.

iv) It is assumed throughout these calculations that each member of the couple has sufficient other assets to fully utilise their nil rate band on death.

v) It is also assumed that neither member of the couple makes any other transfers of value outside the discretionary trust plan.

vi) The above table takes the simplistic view that both members of the couple die at the same time. In reality this is unlikely to be the case, but the table still serves as a fair illustration of the savings which might be achieved.

vii) As explained above, a single individual following the same technique would produce savings equal to half of those shown above.

It is interesting to note that the projected savings start almost immediately, with over £30,000 saved even if the couple die after just one year.

This arises because, once the assets are in the trust, any capital growth is immediately safeguarded from inclusion in your estate.

The savings steadily increase over time but there are significant additional increments in the total saving at each seventh anniversary, as a new nil rate band effectively becomes available.

This table is a perfect illustration of the benefit of starting your Inheritance Tax planning as early as possible.

The main table above is not given in tax terms due to the cashflow impact of ten year anniversary charges which render a direct 'tax paid' comparison slightly unfair.

The comparison is fair for the first ten years, however, as set out below. Later figures are included for illustration only.

Years Survived	Total Tax Paid Using Trust	Total Tax Paid Without Trust	Saving	Saving %
1	433	30,480	30,047	98.6%
2	1,682	59,928	58,246	97.2%
3	3,872	93,281	89,409	95.8%
4	7,210	131,009	123,799	94.5%
5	11,836	173,310	161,474	93.2%
6	17,978	220,721	202,743	91.9%
7	25,323	501,753	476,429	95.0%
8	34,959	595,768	560,809	94.1%
9	47,753	697,745	649,992	93.2%
10	64,199	811,679	747,481	92.1%
15	160,793	1,846,914	1,686,121	91.3%
20	405,391	3,349,989	2,944,598	87.9%
25	793,780	6,204,242	5,410,462	87.2%
30	1,590,867	10,839,287	9,248,420	85.3%

The percentage savings given here are only on **these** assets, not necessarily the couple's entire estate. Nevertheless, the table does ably demonstrate that an excessive concern over anniversary and exit charges is generally unwarranted!

The differences in the 'saving's figures after more than ten years are due to the loss of capital growth arising as a result of payment of ten year anniversary charges.

10.5 HOW TO AVOID ANNIVERSARY AND EXIT CHARGES

Anniversary and exit charges can easily be avoided by:

a) Distributing all trust assets to the beneficiaries before the tenth anniversary of the trust's creation, and
b) Ensuring that the cumulative value of 'relevant transfers' is below the nil rate band at the time the assets are distributed.

Remember that the value of 'relevant transfers' for this purpose includes:

i)   All transfers of value into the trust.
ii) Accumulated income within the trust (see Section 9.15).
iii) Chargeable transfers made in the seven years before setting up the trust (including potentially exempt transfers becoming chargeable on death).
iv) Other settlements made on the day the trust was set up.

We will see a simple example of how anniversary and exit charges may be avoided in Section 10.7.

Even when following the above strategy, up to ten years of 'capital growth' in the value of the trust assets can be accumulated free from Inheritance Tax.

However, in order to achieve the significant longer-term benefits outlined in Section 10.4, or to maintain some of the practical advantages discussed in Section 10.6, it may actually be preferable, in the long run, to suffer ten year anniversary charges.

10.6 WHY NOT JUST GIVE ASSETS DIRECTLY TO THE BENEFICIARIES?

As we know from Chapter 5, assets can be passed directly to other individuals as potentially exempt transfers and all that is required is then to survive seven years to ensure that no Inheritance Tax is payable.

In the right circumstances, this is naturally a much simpler way to avoid Inheritance Tax.

However, using a discretionary trust will often have significant practical advantages over giving assets directly to your ultimate beneficiaries, including

- Control: Although you cannot benefit from the gifted assets (see Section 10.8), you will be able to retain control over them.
- Assets in the discretionary trust are outside any person's estate. This will avoid the danger of unexpected Inheritance Tax liabilities arising if your beneficiaries should pre-decease you.
- Discretionary trusts can be used as a vehicle to 'skip a generation' (or even two) and pass family wealth directly to grandchildren or great-grandchildren, whilst still providing the settlor's children with income during their lifetime.
- The income from, or enjoyment of assets, can be given to your beneficiaries at an early age without exposing them to the risk of losing the underlying capital due to their own inexperience, a bad marriage or some other misfortune.

On top of all these practical issues there is also the fact that assets can be transferred into a discretionary trust free from Capital Gains Tax and we will look at this in the next section.

10.7 HOW TO AVOID INHERITANCE TAX <u>AND</u> CAPITAL GAINS TAX AT THE SAME TIME

As explained in Section 5.10, the transfer of any non-cash assets will generally be treated as a sale of those assets at market value for Capital Gains Tax purposes.

However, because a transfer to a discretionary trust is a chargeable transfer for Inheritance Tax purposes, the transferor is given the ability to 'hold over' any capital gains arising on the assets transferred.

What this means is that no Capital Gains Tax is payable on the transfer and the trust is treated, for Capital Gains Tax purposes, as having acquired the asset at the same price as that originally paid by the transferor.

Furthermore, when, at a later date, the trust then transfers the asset to the ultimate beneficiary, the trustees and the beneficiary may, once again, claim that the capital gain should be 'held over'.

Hence, by this method, appreciating assets may be passed on free of both Inheritance Tax and Capital Gains Tax.

Example

Eric has an investment property worth £291,000 which he wishes to pass to his partner Patty. They are unable to marry and Eric is concerned that he will have a substantial Capital Gains Tax bill if he gives the property directly to Patty.

Instead, therefore, Eric sets up the Slowhand Discretionary Trust with Patty as one of the named beneficiaries. Eric then transfers the property to the trust and elects to hold over the capital gain arising.

Eric has made no previous transfers of value, so he is able to deduct two annual exemptions from the value of the transfer leaving a chargeable transfer of £285,000, which is covered by his nil rate band.

A couple of years later, the trust transfers the property, now worth £350,000, to Patty. Patty and the trustees of the Slowhand Discretionary Trust now jointly elect to hold over the capital gain arising, with the result that Patty is now deemed to have acquired the property for the price which Eric originally paid for it.

There is no exit charge on the transfer to Patty as the nil rate band now exceeds the £291,000 which the property was worth when Eric put it into the trust. The fact that the property is now worth £350,000 is irrelevant.

Points To Note

   i) Only the transferor needs to elect to hold over the gain going into the trust, whereas the trustees and the beneficiary must jointly elect to hold over the gain when the asset is transferred out of the trust.
   ii) Increases in the trust assets' value after transfer into the trust will not give rise to any additional charges as long as those assets are distributed to beneficiaries within ten years.

Wealth Warning

Although the beneficiary is treated as having paid the same price for the transferred asset as the transferor, they are not treated as having acquired it at the same time.

This may result in a significant loss of the available Capital Gains Tax taper relief on the asset.

Furthermore, where gains have been held over in this manner on the transfer of residential property, the beneficiary will not be entitled to any principal private residence relief on the property for Capital Gains Tax purposes.

10.8 LIMITATIONS TO PLANNING WITH DISCRETIONARY TRUSTS

When using discretionary trusts as an Inheritance Tax shelter, it is important to ensure that it is impossible for either the transferor or their spouse to benefit from the trust.

Otherwise, the 'Gift with Reservation' rules (see Section 5.9) will apply, thus rendering the trust ineffective for Inheritance Tax purposes.

Furthermore, from 10th December 2003, this is also imperative from a Capital Gains Tax perspective.

From that date onwards, the general Capital Gains Tax holdover relief for gifts into such a trust (see Section 10.7) ceased to be available where the settlor or their spouse is able to benefit in any way from the recipient trust.

Current proposals are expected to extend the denial of Capital Gains Tax holdover relief to all forms of relevant property trust in which the settlor or their spouse has any interest. Further proposals may also extend the same treatment to any trust where the settlor's minor children are able to benefit.

Such a gift would therefore now give rise to an immediate Capital Gains Tax charge in most cases.

10.9   REVERSIONARY INTEREST TRUSTS

Another very useful type of trust which has been used in Inheritance Tax planning over the last few years is what I will call the 'Reversionary Interest Trust'. These trusts are usually provided by life insurance companies and different companies tend to give their trusts their own different names but the basic principles employed have always been broadly similar.

Whether these types of trust can still be effective in light of the current proposed changes is uncertain, although I am aware of at least one company who have now re-launched a very similar scheme.

A reversionary interest trust is actually not one single trust, but a series of mini-trusts and, prior to 22nd March 2006, it worked something like this:

The Previous Position

The transferor gave a substantial sum to the Reversionary Interest trust, which was then divided up amongst a series of mini-trusts.

Each of the mini-trusts was an interest in possession trust. Transfers into a reversionary interest trust made prior to 22nd March 2006 were thus Potentially Exempt Transfers, which were exempt from Inheritance Tax when the transferor had survived for seven years. The mini-trusts then carried the following rights:

Mini-Trust 1: income to the interest in possession beneficiary for one year, after which the remaining funds in the Trust were paid to the original transferor.

Mini-Trust 2: income to the interest in possession beneficiary for two years, after which the remaining funds in the Trust were paid to the original transferor.

Mini-Trust 3: income to the interest in possession beneficiary for three years, after which the remaining funds in the Trust were paid to the original transferor.

And so on ...

The effect of this was that the transferor continued to receive an 'income' stream from their investment, despite the fact that much of it was no longer in their estate for Inheritance Tax purposes.

The statistical value of their reversionary interests in the mini-trusts did still have to be included in their estate, but this steadily reduced as time passed.

Actually, what the transferor was receiving was not, strictly speaking, income at all, but a return of capital.

This therefore had the added advantage of being free from Income Tax too!

Existing Reversionary Interest Trusts

Existing reversionary interest trusts set up before 22nd March 2006 would appear to still work as long as there is no change to the interest in possession beneficiary.

New Reversionary Interest Trusts

From 22nd March 2006, it may still be possible to set up a reversionary interest trust using absolute trusts (see Section 9.6) in place of interest in possession trusts for the mini-trusts within the reversionary interest trust.

A form of reversionary interest trust using discretionary mini-trusts may also be possible but this would have a maximum ten year lifespan and would also give rise to Inheritance Tax on the original transfer unless restricted in value to the nil rate band.

10.10 LOAN TRUSTS

Another popular scheme provided by most life insurance companies is the 'Loan Trust'.

In essence, the transferor does not make any transfer of value to the trust but simply lends funds to it. As there is no transfer of value, there can be no Inheritance Tax charge.

Funds invested within the trust will (one hopes) experience capital growth but the beauty of this scheme is the fact that the capital growth is outside the original transferor's estate.

All that the original transferor is due is a repayment of the original loan and hence this is the only value remaining in their estate.

There are a number of variations on this scheme.

The transferor may take some income from their loan and this avoids any transfer of value in respect of the interest foregone.

However, it is often possible to argue that the interest foregone is exempt under a combination of the annual exemption and the normal expenditure out of income exemption.

Instead of income, the transferor may progressively withdraw their original loan capital. This capital can be spent on the transferor's own living expenses, thus gradually removing its value from their estate.

Meanwhile, the capital growth and accumulated income within the trust is passed on to the trust beneficiaries and is thus also kept out of the transferor's estate.

A loan trust may be set up as an absolute trust in order to avoid any danger of becoming a relevant property trust. An absolute loan trust would be exempt from any anniversary or exit charges.

Otherwise, as a relevant property trust, there would be some risk of exit and anniversary charges, but these could be avoided by ensuring that the trust assets are distributed before the next ten year anniversary after the trust's net value exceeds the nil rate band.

Chapter 11

Practical Aspects of Inheritance Tax Planning

11.1 THE BIGGER PICTURE

I don't do Inheritance Tax planning, I do 'Estate Preservation' planning.

This is because what is really important is not just saving Inheritance Tax but preserving family wealth for the benefit of the next generation or the taxpayer's other beneficiaries. Saving Inheritance Tax is just one part of preserving wealth and it is important never to lose sight of this bigger picture.

When we come to the bigger issue of estate preservation, there are many other factors to be taken into account. In this chapter we will look at some of these other factors which need to be considered, as well as some other practical aspects of Inheritance Tax planning itself.

11.2 COMMERCIAL ISSUES

From early on in my career I was taught "never to let the tax tail wag the commercial dog". In other words, it is almost always more important to get the commercial aspects right first before letting tax planning dictate your actions.

For example, putting all of your savings into a share of *'Dave's Dodgy Autos'* might be a great way to avoid Inheritance Tax using business property relief, but what's the use of that if Dave runs off to South America with all your money.

After all, when all is said and done, Gordon Brown will only take 40%, so he is (just slightly) better than Dodgy Dave.

On the other hand, as we saw in Section 7.20, saving 40% may still be beneficial overall, even in some slightly uncommercial situations. It's a question of getting the right balance.

This balance is best expressed as follows:

Bayley's Law

"The truly wise taxpayer does not seek merely to minimise the amount of tax paid but rather to maximise the amount of wealth remaining after all taxes have been accounted for."

11.3 INTERACTION WITH OTHER TAXES

After commercial issues, the next most important issue to watch out for is generally other taxes.

When undertaking any tax planning, it is essential to consider all taxes, not just the one that you are trying to save. A saving of 3% Stamp Duty Land Tax at the expense of 17.5% in VAT, for example, is of little benefit!

Inheritance Tax planning will often involve transferring assets and this can have important implications for:

- Capital Gains Tax
- Income Tax
- Corporation Tax
- Stamp Duty (on shares and securities)
- Stamp Duty Land Tax (on land and buildings)
- VAT

The pre-owned assets regime has created a new and complex area of interaction between Inheritance Tax planning and Income Tax which we will be looking at in Chapter 14.

However, the other tax which interacts most frequently and most dramatically with Inheritance Tax has got to be Capital Gains Tax and we will look at that particular 'clash of titans' in Chapter 12.

11.4 JOINTLY HELD PROPERTY

Any form of property can be held jointly, including shares and securities or land and buildings.

The key point to note about jointly held property is that, on a joint owners death, their share may sometimes pass by survivorship and not by intestacy or under the deceased's Will.

This has major implications for Inheritance Tax planning, as you may not be free to transfer your share of jointly held property in the most tax-efficient manner.

Land and Buildings

After the joint bank account, the next most common form of jointly held property in the UK is land and buildings, sometimes referred to as 'real property'. In fact, most couples in the UK now own their home jointly.

In England and Wales, there are two different legal forms for jointly held real property:

- Joint Tenants, or
- Tenants in Common

Joint Tenants

In a joint tenancy the ownership of each person's share passes automatically on death to the other person. This is what is meant by 'survivorship'. Furthermore, neither joint owner is normally able to sell their share of the property without the consent of the other.

This severely restricts the scope for Inheritance Tax planning with the property and joint tenancies are therefore generally less desirable than Tenancies in Common purely from a tax planning perspective. Having said that, however, the security provided by the right of 'survivorship' will often be of more value to many couples.

Tenants in Common

Under a tenancy in common, the joint owners are generally each free to do as they wish with their own share of the property and there is no right of survivorship. The joint owners' shares in the property need not be equal.

A tenancy in common therefore opens up a wide range of Inheritance Tax planning opportunities which are not available under a joint tenancy.

Scotland

In Scotland, joint ownership of real property comes in only one main form called 'Pro Indivisio' ownership and this operates in a broadly similar manner to Tenants in Common.

Practical Implications

As explained above, each person's share in a joint tenancy will usually pass to the other joint owner by survivorship. In the case of the family home, the surviving joint owner will usually be the widow or widower of the deceased and this may therefore be bad Inheritance Tax planning!

A share in property held under a tenancy in common may be passed to anyone, under the terms of the deceased's Will.

Hence, whenever undertaking any Inheritance Tax planning on the family home in England or Wales which involves passing a share of the property to anyone other than the surviving spouse, it will generally first be necessary to ensure that the property is held under a tenancy in common and not a joint tenancy.

Changing the title in property from a joint tenancy to a tenancy in common can be achieved at a reasonably modest cost and should, in itself, be tax free, as it is not treated as a disposal for Capital Gains Tax purposes, nor an acquisition for Stamp Duty Land Tax purposes.

11.5 MORTGAGES

Another important point to be aware of is that any transfer of property which is still subject to a mortgage will require the lender's consent.

If the transferee takes over the mortgage, the outstanding borrowings will be deemed to constitute purchase consideration and may give rise to a Stamp Duty Land Tax charge if they are in excess of £125,000, or £150,000 in the case of commercial property.

11.6 RESIDENTIAL CARE FEES

Whilst Inheritance Tax is a major worry, many people are even more concerned about losing their property to the local authority in order to pay nursing home or residential care fees in their old age.

In some cases, the local authority may even be able to force a sale of a property which has previously been given away if they can show that this was done to avoid payment of the fees.

In some instances, it has been accepted that, where a property has been given away for Inheritance Tax planning purposes, the local authority were unable to claim that the taxpayer's motive was to avoid the care fees.

However, this approach is not entirely reliable, as many families have found to their cost (see further in Section 12.7).

A better approach is often to take out long term care insurance or even emergency care assurance. The latter approach generally requires the payment of a single lump sum premium in exchange for an annuity covering the residential care fees.

The amount of the premium is generally equal to around two to three years' worth of the care fees.

Emergency care assurance is a useful strategy employed by many families who wish to have certainty about the cost of looking after their elderly relative.

If necessary, the premium can be funded by way of a loan secured against the relative's former home, thus enabling the family to keep the property and perhaps even benefit from the Capital Gains Tax uplift on death (see Section 12.1).

11.7   WILLS AND INTESTACY

Most of us know we should make a Will, but a great many of us put it off until it's too late. (It's still on my 'to do' list, I must admit.)

Quite apart from any Inheritance Tax planning, a Will is sensible as, without a valid Will, your assets will be divided up according to the ancient laws of intestacy and this may well be very different to what you would have liked.

More importantly, a Will is essential for nominating the future guardians of your children if, as Oscar Wilde would have put it, they are careless enough to lose both parents.

Dying Without a Will

Most people are pretty relaxed about dying intestate (without a Will) until they realise what would actually happen.

In the tables which follow, 'Issue' generally means your children but, if your children pre-decease you, their children will take their place.

For example, if you have three children and one of them pre-deceases you, leaving two children of their own, the share going to 'your children' will be divided so that one third of that share goes to each of your surviving children and one sixth of that share goes to each of your grandchildren by your deceased child.

Dying Without a Will: England and Wales

If you are domiciled in England and Wales, and die without a Will, your estate will be divided up as follows:

1. If you leave a spouse (or civil partner) and issue.

The first £125,000 and all personal possessions go to your spouse. 50% of the balance is divided equally between your children.

The remaining 50% is held on trust, with your spouse having a life interest and the remainder going to your children.

2. If you leave a spouse (or civil partner) but no issue.

If you have no surviving parents, siblings, nephews or nieces, your entire estate goes to your spouse.

Otherwise, your spouse's share is restricted to £200,000 and all personal possessions, plus 50% of the remaining balance.

The other 50% of the balance goes to your parents if they survive you, to your siblings if both of your parents pre-decease you, or to your nephews and nieces if your siblings also pre-decease you.

3. If you leave issue but no spouse (or civil partner).

Your estate is divided equally between your children.

4. If you leave no spouse (or civil partner) or issue.

Your estate goes to the nearest relatives to survive you, based on the following order of priorities:

- i) Your parents
- ii) Your siblings, or their issue (i.e. your nieces and nephews)
- iii) Your grandparents
- iv) Your aunts and uncles

5. If no near-relatives survive you.

Your entire estate goes to the Crown!

Dying Without a Will: Scotland

If you are domiciled in Scotland, and die without a Will, your estate will be divided up as follows:

1. If you leave a spouse (or civil partner) and issue.

Your spouse gets:
 i)   Your interest in any dwelling (i.e. the family home) up to a value of £300,000. If the family home's value exceeds this amount, the spouse's entitlement is limited to the right to receive the sum of £300,000.
 ii) Personal possessions up to the value of £24,000.
 iii) The first £42,000 of the remaining estate.
 iv) One third of any other moveable property (i.e. anything other than land and buildings).

Your children then get the remainder of your estate.

2. If you leave a spouse (or civil partner) but no issue.

Your spouse gets:

 i)   Your interest in any dwelling (i.e. the family home) up to a value of £300,000. If the family home's value exceeds this amount, the spouse's entitlement is limited to the right to receive the sum of £300,000.

 ii) Personal possessions up to the value of £24,000.

 iii) The first £75,000 of the remaining estate.

 iv) One half of any other moveable property (i.e. anything other than land and buildings).

The rest of your estate falls into your 'free estate' and is dealt with as detailed below. If you have no surviving parents, siblings or issue of your siblings, your spouse will effectively receive your entire estate.

3. If you leave issue but no spouse (or civil partner).

Your estate is divided equally between your children.

4. If you leave no spouse (or civil partner) or issue.

Your entire estate will now be dealt with under the rules for a 'free estate'.

Free Estate

In dealing with your free estate, any claimant's children or remoter issue may take the place of a claimant who has pre-deceased you, except where the deceased claimant was your spouse or parent.

If you are survived by both parents and siblings (or their issue), 50% of your free estate goes to your parent and 50% to your siblings or their issue. In any other case, the free estate goes to the nearest relatives to survive you, based on the following order of priorities:

i) Your siblings
ii) Your parents
iii) Your surviving spouse (for cases under (2) above)
iv) Uncles and aunts
v) Grandparents
vi) Grandparents' siblings
vii) Great-grandparents, etc.

If you have no relatives, as set out above; yes, you've guessed it, everything goes to the Crown.

So, as you can see, whether you live in Swansea, Penzance or Aberdeen (and probably Belfast too, although I don't have those rules available), you really shouldn't be relaxed about dying without a Will.

It is not uncommon for widows to be forced to sell the family home due to the operation of the above rules and, as I pointed out previously, without proper provision, children may also end up being taken into care.

The statutory rules set out above take no account of common-law partners, step-children or many other important personal relationships. A remote cousin could get everything in priority to a fondly loved step-child!

The Crown could even get your house in priority to your best friend or even a common-law partner who you've lived with for decades. And you thought Inheritance Tax was bad enough at 40%!

OK, sermon over.

(And I really must get around to doing *my* Will.)

11.8 STATUTORY RIGHTS

In England, Wales or Northern Ireland, you may generally distribute your entire estate as you wish under the terms of your Will.

Surviving spouses may, however apply to the courts for an increased share of the estate where the amount already provided to them in the Will does not represent adequate financial provision for their care and maintenance. In essence, this is something akin to posthumous divorce proceedings.

Similar applications may be made on behalf of dependent minor children of the deceased.

A different system operates in Scotland where 'legal rights' will take priority over the terms of the deceased's Will unless waived by the beneficiaries concerned.

Legal rights for beneficiaries of a deceased domiciled in Scotland are as follows:

Surviving spouse: Where there are no issue of the deceased, one half of the deceased's moveable property, otherwise one third.

Surviving issue: Where there is no surviving spouse of the deceased, one half of the deceased's moveable property, otherwise one third.

Remember, the question of whether you are domiciled in Scotland is the same as any other domicile issue (see Chapter 16). Hence, you may have lived in London for many decades, but, if you or your parents were born in Scotland, you could still be domiciled in Scotland and your spouse and children will still have 'legal rights' as set out above.

11.9 LIFE ASSURANCE

One simple way to ensure that your estate is not excessively inflated on your death is to ensure that any life assurance policies which you take out are written into trust for the benefit of other family members.

In that way, the proceeds of the policies will never fall into your estate but will go, instead, to your intended beneficiaries free of Inheritance Tax.

By using a trust, you will be able to vary the intended beneficiaries over the course of your lifetime.

Ideally, if they can afford to do without it, your spouse or civil partner should not be the beneficiary under any of your life assurance policies.

As mentioned previously, it would be wise to try to get all forms of life insurance cover which you have written into trust and thus excluded from your estate.

This should also extend to the 'Death Benefit' under any pension schemes, where possible.

Wealth Warning

The life insurance industry is concerned that the current proposed changes to the Inheritance Tax treatment of trusts (see Chapter 9) may result in the imposition of anniversary charges on certain trusts holding life policies for the benefit of the policyholder's family.

However, Revenue & Customs have made some assurances that this is not what is intended by the new proposed legislation and it is therefore to be hoped that no such charges will arise in practice. Watch this space on this one!

11.10 INSURING FOR INHERITANCE TAX LIABILITIES

Much of the Inheritance Tax planning discussed elsewhere in this guide depends on the transferor surviving for a certain period after a transfer, or some other transaction, has been made. Often the period concerned will be seven years, but survival to other anniversaries can often also be critical.

When death occurs before the expiry of the critical period, unexpected tax bills can often arrive as a nasty surprise.

It is often a good idea, therefore, to take out some term life insurance on the transferor to guard against this possibility.

Wealth Warning

Make sure that the transferor themselves is not the beneficiary of the term insurance as this will, once again, inflate the value of their estate and lead to an effective 'grossing up' of Inheritance Tax liabilities.

11.11 PENSIONS

This time last year there was a great deal of excitement at the prospect that the new pensions regime commencing on 6th April 2006 ('A Day') would provide some new Inheritance Tax planning opportunities in the shape of the new 'Alternatively Secured Pension' arrangements.

However, as many of us had anticipated, new proposed legislation announced in the Budget on 22nd March 2006 is now expected to effectively remove any Inheritance Tax advantages under 'Alternatively Secured Pension' arrangements. Doubtlessly, some loopholes will still remain but, at present, it's too early to tell what these will be.

11.12 LOTTERY SYNDICATES

Lottery and pools syndicates are 'breeding grounds' for potential Inheritance Tax problems. Just imagine this:

Example

Donny wins £15m on the National Lottery. It's in all the newspapers, so you can bet that Revenue & Customs know about it.

He gives £3m to each of his brothers, Wayne, Merrill, Jay and Jimmy.

Tragically, just a few weeks later, Donny is killed whilst water skiing in Utah.

Revenue & Customs demand almost £6m in Inheritance Tax from Donny's family as the transfers made to his brothers were made only a few weeks before his death.

"But we were in a syndicate" protest the brothers. "Prove it!" replies Revenue & Customs.

Ouch!

The simple answer to this problem, of course, is to make sure that you have documentary evidence of any syndicate arrangements.

We can also take the principle of the lottery syndicate one step further.

Recently, I heard on the radio that an 84 year-old lottery winner had given away his entire £13m win to a combination of charities and family and friends.

Like most other people (I suspect), my first thought was "what a nice chap", but then the cynic in me took over and I began to wonder if there was perhaps an Inheritance Tax planning motive present here.

But, at 84, our lottery winner's life expectancy is around five and a half years. Hence, whilst his charitable transferees are already in the clear, his family and friends would be well advised to keep 40% of their gifts to one side in case their benefactor doesn't last too long.

Our winner could, however, have planned things better.

Let's suppose that he had previously drawn up a lottery syndicate agreement with his family and friends and agreed to share any winnings with them. Naturally, his family and friends would also agree to contribute to the weekly lottery stake. However, in practice, the transferor would then pay the weekly stake himself.

The transferor's payment of the weekly stake would represent a transfer of value but it should be sufficiently small to be exempt as 'normal expenditure out of income' or else to be covered by the annual exemption or the small gifts exemption.

I would suggest that this course of action would make sense for any elderly person playing the lottery (or 'doing the pools', etc.).

Chapter 12

Interaction With Capital Gains Tax

12.1 THE UPLIFT ON DEATH

Do you remember my opening comments in Section 5.5? I'll refresh your memory:

"For Capital Gains Tax purposes, death is often a very good tax-planning strategy."

The reason for this rather black-humoured remark is one simple fact. On death, the base cost of all the deceased's assets is uplifted to their market value at that date.

Example

In 1955, Jerry set up Killer Limited with an investment of just £1,000.

In 1982, Jerry's Killer Limited shares are worth £500,000 and, by January 2007, his controlling interest in Killer Promotions PLC (the same company) is worth £100m. Even after taper relief and his annual exemption, Jerry's Capital Gains Tax bill on a sale of these shares would be almost £26m.

Sadly, however, Jerry dies in January 2007 and leaves his entire Killer Promotions PLC shareholding to his son Lee. Lee sells the shares for £102m in April 2007. His Capital Gains Tax bill will be just £800,000 (ignoring his annual exemption).

Lee is treated as if he acquired the shares in January 2007 for a price of £100m. We call this the Capital Gains Tax 'uplift on death'. His taxable gain on the sale in April is therefore just £2m.

The bad news for Lee, however, is the fact that he is not entitled to any taper relief on his sale of the shares despite the fact that Jerry had held them for over 50 years. Well, you can't win them all!

12.2 THE CAPITAL GAINS TAX vs INHERITANCE TAX DILEMMA

Whilst death is very good Capital Gains Tax planning, lifetime transfers generally pose a problem.

As explained in Section 5.10, a lifetime transfer of anything other than cash (in sterling) will give rise to a Capital Gains Tax disposal which is deemed to take place at market value.

Hence, in our example in Section 12.2, if Jerry had given the Killer Promotions PLC shares to Lee before he died, he would have given himself a £26m Capital Gains Tax bill!

This creates a bit of a dilemma.

The best way to avoid Inheritance Tax is often to make lifetime transfers whereas the best way to avoid Capital Gains Tax is to hold on to assets until death.

Obviously, what we really want to do is to minimise the overall tax burden (or, to be more precise, to follow *Bayley's Law* – as per Section 11.2).

To do this, we need to start by considering what reliefs the assets concerned will qualify for, both under the Inheritance Tax regime and the Capital Gains Tax regime. The three major areas to consider are:

- Business Assets
- Transfers to spouses
- The family home

We will now take a look at each of these areas in turn. 'Other assets' which do not fall under any of these headings are dealt with in Section 12.8.

12.3 BUSINESS ASSETS

As we have already seen, the uplift on death provides an enormous potential to save Capital Gains Tax. Whether that saving is achieved at an Inheritance Tax cost, however, is partly dependent on the interaction between business property relief and its Capital Gains Tax equivalent, business asset taper relief.

Where assets qualify as business assets for Capital Gains Tax purposes, taper relief provides exemption from Capital Gains Tax on 75% of the capital gain arising on a disposal of those assets by a person who has held them for two years or more. This produces an effective maximum Capital Gains Tax rate of just 10% for qualifying business assets after two years.

For qualifying business assets held for at least one year, but less than two, taper relief is given at 50%.

Where assets do not qualify as business assets for Capital Gains Tax purposes, taper relief is given at much lower rates. Broadly, the rate of taper relief for non-business assets is just 5% after three years of ownership, plus an additional 5% for each year thereafter until the relief reaches a maximum level of 40% after ten years of ownership.

For a full definition of 'business assets' for Capital Gains Tax purposes see the Taxcafe guide *How To Avoid Property Tax*.

In our example in Section 12.1, I assumed that the shares in Killer Promotions PLC did not qualify as business assets for Capital Gains Tax taper relief purposes. This resulted in an enormous potential Capital Gains Tax bill for Jerry.

If, however, those same shares did qualify for business property relief (see Chapter 7), Jerry would have been able to leave them to Lee free of Inheritance Tax. As we saw in Section 12.1, Lee was then treated as if he had bought the shares at market value at the date of Jerry's death, thus drastically reducing his potential Capital Gains Tax bill.

This is therefore a prime example of a situation where holding on to the assets until death is preferable.

Make No Assumptions About Taper Relief

Most assets which qualify for business asset taper relief for Capital Gains Tax will probably also qualify for business property relief for

Inheritance Tax. One major exception to this, however, is commercial investment property and this is not the only one.

The converse is even less true, as business property relief is often available under the 'wholly or mainly' rule (see Section 7.7), whereas the general rule for business asset taper relief requires the underlying business not to include any 'substantial' element of non-trading activities. As we saw in Section 7.16, this is usually taken to mean that non-trading activities amount to no more than 20% of the business, using any of the tests set out in Section 7.7.

However, despite the fact that these two important reliefs operate under different sets of rules, the interaction between them has enormous consequences for estate preservation planning. There are four possible combinations for the two reliefs, so let's examine each in turn.

Both Business Property Relief and Business Asset Taper Relief Available

The assets can be passed on free from Inheritance Tax. Maximum Capital Gains Tax taper relief will be restored after two years if the transferee qualifies. It therefore often makes sense for the transferor to hang on to these assets and transfer them on death to obtain the Capital Gains Tax uplift with no Inheritance Tax cost.

If it is not possible to hang on to the original assets until death, the same result can sometimes be achieved by exchanging these assets for 'replacement assets', as explained in Section 7.12. To avoid any Capital Gains Tax liabilities on the exchange, the 'replacement assets' generally need to be one of the following:

   i)   Shares issued in exchange for shares in the transferor's own company (e.g. a 'takeover').

   ii) Shares issued in exchange for the transfer of an unincorporated business into a company.

   iii) Business property acquired within the three year period following the disposal of the original assets. (eg buying a business property to replace an old one used in the same business or the acquisition of property for use in a new qualifying business.)

Any new business under (iii) above will also need to qualify as a trading business for Capital Gains Tax purposes.

Assets which qualify for business asset taper relief can also generally be transferred during the transferor's lifetime without any Capital Gains Tax liability due to the availability of holdover relief on 'Gifts of Business Assets' (see Section 12.4).

Whilst this avoids Capital Gains Tax on the transfer, however, it also denies the transferee the benefit of the 'uplift on death'.

Business Property Relief Is Available But Not Business Asset Taper Relief

The assets can be passed on free from Inheritance Tax. It will take ten years for the transferee to obtain 40% taper relief for Capital Gains Tax purposes.

In many cases it will make sense to hang on to these assets and only transfer them on death, where possible. Capital Gains Tax uplift will be obtained and both Inheritance Tax and Capital Gains Tax can be avoided when the transferee sells the assets shortly afterwards.

At the very least, there should be a very substantial reduction in Capital Gains Tax, as we saw in Section 12.1.

Again, it may be possible to achieve the same results when the assets are exchanged for 'replacement assets' before death.

However, the opportunity to avoid Capital Gains Tax on such an exchange is more limited and only items (i) and (ii) outlined above will now be sufficient for this purpose.

Lifetime transfers of these assets are likely to give rise to immediate Capital Gains Tax liabilities.

Business Asset Taper Relief Is Available But Not Business Property Relief

This may initially seem like the least likely of our four scenarios, but it does happen, the major example being commercial investment property.

We now have a major dilemma. A sale or transfer of the assets before death will give rise to a maximum Capital Gains Tax charge of just 10%, but the opportunity to achieve the Capital Gains Tax uplift will be lost. Either way, whether the assets themselves or the sale proceeds are held at the time of death, Inheritance Tax will be fully chargeable.

Furthermore, where business property relief is not available, it is unlikely that the assets will be eligible for holdover relief on 'Gifts of Business Assets' (see Section 12.4).

In practice, it may be difficult to establish the best course of action but an early transfer will often produce an overall saving.

Example

Sanjeev has a commercial investment property which he acquired in May 2000 for £600,000. He has been letting the property to qualifying unquoted trading companies ever since and hence he is entitled to 75% taper relief on it.

In June 2006, he transfers the property to his daughter Meera when it is worth £1m. As a higher rate taxpayer, his resultant Capital Gains Tax bill is £36,480 after taper relief and his annual exemption.

In July 2013, Sanjeev dies when the property is worth £1.8m. As the transfer to Meera took place more than seven years previously, no Inheritance Tax is due.

If Sanjeev had still held the property at this time, the Inheritance Tax arising would have been between £575,600 and £720,000, depending on whether he had used up his nil rate band elsewhere. (I have estimated the nil rate band for 2013/2014 at £361,000.)

Meera now sells the property and she herself ends up with a Capital Gains Tax bill of £75,640 after taper relief and her 2013/2014 annual exemption of, say, £10,900. (She is also a higher rate taxpayer.)

Hence, whilst father and daughter between them have paid £112,120 in Capital Gains Tax, the overall net tax saving for the family is at least £463,480.

Clearly, in this example, it was worth incurring a relatively small Capital Gains Tax cost, as the investment property was successfully removed from Sanjeev's estate by way of a potentially exempt transfer more than seven years before his death.

If Sanjeev had died immediately after his transfer to Meera, however, there would have been no Inheritance Tax saving and the Capital Gains Tax liability would have been incurred needlessly when she could have had a Capital Gains Tax uplift on her father's death.

Between these two extremes lie an almost infinite variety of outcomes. However, as a general guide, I have produced the table below.

This table follows broadly the same lines as the example, but with a few minor modifications. It is based on the following assumptions:

i) There is an existing gain of £400,000 giving rise to a Capital Gains Tax liability of £36,480 (as in our example).

ii) The property is currently worth £1m and its future value will increase at a rate of 7.5% per annum (compound).

iii) The property will qualify for business asset taper relief in the transferee's hands.

iv) The transferee will sell the property immediately after the transferor's death.

v) The nil rate band and the Capital Gains Tax annual exemption will increase in line with inflation at the rate of 2.5% per annum.

vi) The nil rate band would be utilised against the property if it were still in the transferor's estate.

vii) The transferor survives just beyond the relevant anniversary.

Transferor Dies After	Property Value on Death	Inheritance Tax on Transfer	Capital Gains Tax on Final Sale	Inheritance Tax if Still in Estate	Net Saving or (Cost)*
< 1 year	1,000,000	£286,000	£0	£286,000	(£36,480)
1 year	1,075,000	£280,000	£11,360	£310,000	(£17,840)
2 years	1,155,625	£275,200	£11,803	£337,450	£13,968
3 years	1,242,297	£216,000	£20,350	£366,919	£94,089
4 years	1,335,469	£159,840	£29,547	£400,588	£174,721
5 years	1,435,629	£105,120	£39,443	£437,052	£256,009
6 years	1,543,302	£51,840	£50,090	£476,521	£338,110
7 years	1,659,049	£0	£61,545	£519,220	£421,195
8 years	1,783,478	£0	£73,868	£564,991	£454,643
9 years	1,917,239	£0	£87,124	£614,495	£490,892
10 years	2,061,032	£0	£101,383	£668,013	£530,149

* - the net saving/(cost) takes account of the Capital Gains Tax paid on the original transfer.

As we can see, under this scenario, the transferor only needs to survive for two years to make the transfer worthwhile.

Neither Business Property Relief nor Business Asset Taper Relief Available

Our fourth category is basically non-business assets. We will return to these in Section 12.8.

12.4   GIFTS OF BUSINESS ASSETS

Sadly, despite its name, this relief does not actually apply to assets used in a 'business', but only to assets used in a trade. What will qualify as a 'trade' can be very difficult to define, but it certainly does not include any property investment businesses.

Furthermore, anything which does not qualify for business property relief will probably not qualify for this relief.

Hence, we are generally talking about assets which qualify for both business property relief and business asset taper relief.

Broadly, the assets which qualify will be:

- Assets used in a qualifying trade.
- Unquoted shares in a trading company.
- A holding of at least 5% of a quoted trading company.

This time, 'unquoted' does not include shares traded on the Unlisted Securities Market or AIM.

To be a trading company, we again need to follow the 20% test which also applies for business asset taper relief (see Section 12.3).

Where a qualifying asset is transferred by way of gift, the capital gain arising may be held over. This provides an effective deferral of any Capital Gains Tax but it does mean that the uplift on death will be lost.

Example

Kurt set up Nevermind Limited in 1998 with a share capital of just 100 £1 ordinary shares. The shares qualify for both business property relief and business asset taper relief.

In December 2006, Kurt gives 25 shares to Courtney and elects to hold over the capital gain arising. In effect, this means that Courtney is treated as if she acquired the shares for £1 each: the same price that Kurt paid for them.

Kurt dies in March 2007 and, fearing a drop in value, Courtney decides to sell her Nevermind Limited shares at their current value of £50,000 per share, or £1.25m in total.

Courtney's base cost for her shares is just £25, so she ends up with a capital gain of £1,249,975. Unfortunately, as she herself has held the shares for less than two years, she will not be entitled to any taper relief and her Capital Gains Tax bill is therefore £496,470.

In the example, Courtney sold up because she feared a drop in value. This made commercial sense and I would not argue with it. In other cases, however, it will generally make sense to retain the transferred assets for at least two years in order to get 75% taper relief.

Holdover relief on 'Gifts of Business Assets' is not available for:

- A transfer of shares or securities to a company.
- Any transfer to a trust from which the transferor and their spouse are not totally excluded from any benefit.

12.5 TRANSFERS TO SPOUSES

As we know, transfers to your spouse are usually exempt from Inheritance Tax.

Furthermore, subject to the wealth warning below, transfers to your spouse are also usually exempt from Capital Gains Tax.

However, only transfers on death will benefit from the Capital Gains Tax uplift explained in Section 12.1.

It therefore makes sense to hold on to any assets which are subject to Capital Gains Tax and which you ultimately intend to leave to your spouse so that they can benefit from the uplift on death.

Furthermore, a transfer of assets to your spouse prior to their death could be used to get a Capital Gains Tax uplift on their death.

You need to be sure that the assets are going to come back to you though!

Wealth Warning

Unlike the Inheritance Tax exemption, the Capital Gains Tax exemption for transfers between spouses ceases to apply at the end of the tax year in which they separate.

Separated couples who have not yet obtained a decree absolute are therefore eligible for the Inheritance Tax relief but not the Capital Gains Tax relief.

12.6 CAPITAL GAINS TAX AND THE FAMILY HOME

I could write an entire chapter on this subject alone. In fact, I have, but that chapter already appears in the Taxcafe guide *How To Avoid Property Tax*.

To put it simply though, your own home is exempt from Capital Gains Tax for as long as you live in it as your only or main residence and for at least three years thereafter. Full exemption will generally apply as long as you moved into the property within one year of acquisition. Any other periods of absence, however, may result in a partial loss of your exemption.

Each married couple or single individual may have just one main residence for Capital Gains Tax purposes at any given time.

Sadly, however, as far as the Government are concerned, the family home does not seem to merit any Inheritance Tax exemption. We will therefore look at Inheritance Tax planning for the family home in the next chapter.

Nevertheless, as far as Capital Gains Tax is concerned, any lifetime transfer of your qualifying main residence whilst you are still living there, or within the next three years thereafter, will be exempt.

So, what's the problem?

Well, apart from all the Inheritance Tax problems which we will look at in the next chapter, there are two main Capital Gains Tax problems with giving away your main residence:

- The transferees will lose the ability to benefit from the Capital Gains Tax uplift on death, and
- Unless they move into the property, the transferees will also lose any main residence exemption on the property.

In essence, the transferees will be treated for Capital Gains Tax purposes as having acquired the house at its market value at the date of transfer and will be exposed to Capital Gains Tax on any growth in value thereafter.

Practical Implications

A sale of the parent's home at any time within three years of them ceasing to occupy it as their main residence would generally be fully exempt from Capital Gains Tax if they were still the owner at that time.

Furthermore, if the parent retained the property until their death, it would be subject to the uplift on death, giving the children a complete exemption from any gain arising during the parent's lifetime, even if the parent had been absent from the property for more than three years.

Conversely, if a child owns their parent's current or former home, but does not occupy it as their own main residence themselves, it is effectively treated like an investment property and is fully exposed to Capital Gains Tax on a subsequent sale. The capital gain in such cases will then be based on the property's value at the time that the child acquired it and not at the time of the parent's death. The relevant transfer may be several years earlier when the property's value was many thousands of pounds less.

The interplay between Capital Gains Tax and Inheritance Tax on the family home can produce one of three results:

i) The Inheritance Tax saving may outweigh the Capital Gains Tax exposure which has been created. This is fine and means that the planning is still worthwhile.

ii) The Inheritance Tax saving comes at the price of an equal, or similar, level of potential Capital Gains Tax liability. Such instances may still be worthwhile, as they may still produce a significant cashflow saving by deferring the tax arising. (This will often be the case where the beneficiaries have no intention of ever selling the property, or at least not for some considerable time.)

iii) The Inheritance Tax saving results in a significantly greater amount of potential Capital Gains Tax. This, clearly, would be foolhardy if the beneficiaries are contemplating any sale of the property in the foreseeable future.

If the total value of the parent's estate does not significantly exceed the nil rate band, it will probably make sense for them to retain ownership of the former family home, if possible, as the advantage of the Capital Gains Tax uplift on death is likely to outweigh any Inheritance Tax cost.

Wealth Warning

Where the parent still resides in the property, any transfer will usually be a 'Gift with Reservation' (although we will see some exceptions to this in the next chapter).

As we shall see in the next section, it would generally be wise to refrain from making any transfer which would be a 'Gift with Reservation', as there would be no Inheritance Tax advantage but all of the Capital Gains Tax disadvantages would remain.

12.7 CAPITAL GAINS TAX AND GIFTS WITH RESERVATION

As explained in Section 5.9, when a transfer falls foul of the 'Gifts with Reservation' rules, it will be ineffective until such time as the relevant 'reservation' comes to an end.

This has absolutely no impact whatsoever on the Capital Gains Tax treatment of the asset. The transfer which was subject to a 'Gift with Reservation' may still give rise to Capital Gains Tax liabilities based on the market value of the asset transferred and the new legal owner of the transferred asset will lose the benefit of any reliefs to which the transferor may have been entitled, including taper relief and main residence relief on the transferor's own home.

Generally, with few exceptions, this situation should be avoided as it usually creates Capital Gains Tax problems without saving any Inheritance Tax.

Example

In late 1999, Tina gave her house to her son, Robert, but continued to live there until 2006, when she moved into a nursing home. The house was worth £150,000 in 1999 but had increased in value to £500,000 by 2006.

Tragically, Tina dies in March 2007, leaving only a few small possessions with no material value and just enough cash to pay her last month's nursing home fees and her funeral expenses.

However, as she only moved out of her house in 2006, its value at that date must be brought back into her estate, thus resulting in an Inheritance Tax bill of £86,000.

To help pay the Inheritance Tax, Robert sells the house, which, due to neglect, has fallen slightly in value to £480,000. However, for Capital Gains Tax purposes, he is treated as having acquired the house for just £150,000, thus giving rise to a Capital Gains Tax bill of £95,480, on top of the Inheritance Tax bill.

I have seen this type of situation countless times and it's an absolute tragedy.

Had Tina simply held on to the house, Robert would have paid just £78,000 in Inheritance Tax on her death and little or no Capital Gains Tax at all. The transfer in 1999 has effectively cost Robert more than £100,000 in unnecessary extra tax.

Many families have attempted this type of planning to their cost. To make it even worse, many of these transfers were done to avoid paying residential care fees (see Section 11.6) but, as a result of a number of rule changes and successful cases taken by the local authorities, this part of the plan has usually failed as well.

In the vast majority of cases, therefore, transfers which are gifts with reservation are to be avoided like the plague!

12.8 OTHER ASSETS

So what about those other assets, which do not qualify as business assets or main residences and which you're not planning to give to your spouse?

Well, here we need to go back to our fourth scenario from Section 12.3, i.e. no business property relief and no business asset taper relief.

This will mean that the loss of the Capital Gains Tax uplift on death will make a prior transfer of the property even less attractive. Nevertheless, the opportunity to save Inheritance Tax by way of an early lifetime transfer remains.

To illustrate the position, let's revisit our 'Sanjeev and Meera' example, but now we'll assume that the asset being transferred does not qualify for business asset taper relief.

Example

As before, let's assume that Sanjeev has an investment property which he acquired in May 2000 for £600,000. However, we will now assume that he has been letting the property to a quoted company and that he is therefore only entitled to non-business asset taper relief on it.

As before, in June 2006, he transfers the property to his daughter Meera when it is worth £1m. As a higher rate taxpayer, his Capital Gains Tax bill on this transfer will be £124,480. (His gain is £400,000, which is reduced to £311,200 after taper relief at 20% and his annual exemption of £8,800.)

Making all of the same assumptions as we made in Section 12.3, except for the fact that business asset taper relief is not available, the position will be as follows:

Transferor Dies After	Property Value on Death	Inheritance Tax on Transfer	Capital Gains Tax on Final Sale	Inheritance Tax if Still in Estate	Net Saving or (Cost)
< 1 year	1,000,000	£286,000	£0	£286,000	(£124,480)
1 year	1,075,000	£280,000	£26,360	£310,000	(£120,840)
2 years	1,155,625	£275,200	£58,490	£337,450	(£120,720)
3 years	1,242,297	£216,000	£88,193	£366,919	(£61,754)
4 years	1,335,469	£159,840	£116,769	£400,588	(£501)
5 years	1,435,629	£105,120	£143,994	£437,052	£63,458
6 years	1,543,302	£51,840	£169,616	£476,521	£130,584
7 years	1,659,049	£0	£193,355	£519,220	£201,385
8 years	1,783,478	£0	£214,894	£564,991	£225,617
9 years	1,917,239	£0	£233,882	£614,495	£256,133
10 years	2,061,032	£0	£249,928	£668,013	£293,605

As we can see, in this example, the transfer only becomes worthwhile when the transferor survives for five years.

The position will, of course, be different when the transferee holds onto the property after the transferor's death and thus accumulates a better rate of taper relief.

12.9 CAPITAL GAINS TAX AND TRUSTS

In Chapter 9, we considered the various different types of trust and saw that some of them had their own 'separate life' for Inheritance Tax purposes and some did not.

With the single exception of bare trusts, all other trusts are treated as a separate legal entity for Capital Gains Tax purposes.

This effectively means that, subject to any other exemptions which may be available:

- Transfers into a trust are treated as disposals made at market value, and
- Transfers to beneficiaries from a trust are again treated as disposals at market value.

In the case of a bare trust, it is only the transfer to the trust which represents a disposal for Capital Gains Tax purposes. Thereafter, the assets of the trust are treated as belonging to the beneficiary for the purposes of both Inheritance Tax and Capital Gains Tax.

Prior to 22nd March 2006, assets held in an interest in possession trust usually qualified for the Capital Gains Tax uplift on the death of the beneficiary. This will no longer apply when the trust falls into the relevant property trust regime.

Chapter 13

The Family Home

13.1 WHEN OUR MAIN ASSET BECOMES OUR MAIN LIABILITY

For most of us, the family home is our major asset and, in many cases, it is also the main cause of Inheritance Tax liabilities.

As already mentioned in Section 5.9, the major stumbling block to effective Inheritance Tax planning in respect of the family home is caused by the 'Gifts With Reservation' provisions.

Furthermore, whenever the transferor of *any* asset (but, most particularly, the family home) continues to enjoy the benefit of that asset after 5th April 2005, there will now also be an Income Tax charge on the 'benefit-in-kind'.

The possible application of that charge, known as the 'Pre-Owned Asset Charge', to the planning methods discussed in this chapter is examined in detail in Chapter 14.

Nevertheless, despite these drawbacks, there are still a number of potential methods for avoiding or reducing the Inheritance Tax on the family home.

13.2 MOVE OUT AND THEN GIVE IT AWAY

If you can afford to, and you are willing to do it, you can simply move out of the house and then give it away.

The gift is a Potentially Exempt Transfer which will escape any Inheritance Tax as long as you survive seven years.

Furthermore, as long as you make the gift within three years of the date you move out of the house, it will also be exempt from Capital Gains Tax under the Principal Private Residence relief rules.

If you are prepared to do this, you could then move into rented accommodation, or buy a more modest house, with a value below the nil rate band.

This method will not suit everyone, but it is worth considering in some cases.

13.3   SELL UP AND GIVE AWAY THE PROCEEDS

If you can't quite afford to follow the above strategy, you could, instead, sell your current home, buy a smaller one with a value below the nil rate band and then give away the surplus left over cash. All you need to do then is just to survive another seven years.

If you're feeling really brave, you could even give away all the sale proceeds and move into rented property. Whilst this is good Inheritance Tax planning, it doesn't leave you with much security in your old age and it might cause some problems with the local authority later if you ever need to go into a residential home.

13.4   RE-MORTGAGE AND GIVE AWAY THE PROCEEDS

If you would prefer to stay in your current home, another way to get most of its value out of your estate, without having to move out of it, is to re-mortgage the property and then give away or spend the borrowed funds.

The outstanding mortgage balance will be deducted from your estate when you die and this will reduce your Inheritance Tax bill as long as you have either:

- Given away the borrowed funds and then survived seven years, or
- Spent the borrowed funds before you die.

The major drawback here is the need to service the mortgage debt from your retirement income.

13.5   RE-MORTGAGE AND BUY AN ANNUITY

A refinement to the above is to buy an annuity with some or all of the re-mortgage proceeds. This will enable you to service the debt and give away or spend any surplus.

The drawback here is that in the event of a premature death shortly after purchasing the annuity, a lot of your home's value will have been lost – not to Her Majesty's Treasury but to the annuity provider.

13.6   SALE AT MARKET VALUE

If you sell your house to your children, or other beneficiaries, at full market value, no 'transfer of value' can have taken place and hence, thereafter, the property will no longer be within your estate for Inheritance Tax purposes.

Wealth Warning

Any prior arrangement to give any part of the sale proceeds back to the purchaser will render this planning void, since the sale would not then have taken place on 'arm's length terms', as required, and a transfer of value will have taken place. Furthermore, there must not be any obligation on the purchaser's part to allow you to continue to occupy the property.

The second point above means that you will subsequently only be able to live in the property under an informal 'licence to occupy', which is totally at the purchaser's whim. This will not suit everyone!

Readers may wonder what Inheritance Tax saving this method will actually generate. There are two points to note:

i) You are free to spend the sale proceeds, perhaps to support yourself in your retirement.

ii) Any further growth in the property's value is safely excluded from your estate.

As you spend the proceeds and the property grows in value, the reduction in your taxable estate starts to accumulate.

These savings also start immediately after the sale, and it is not necessary to survive for any period to benefit from them.

In an era of increasing property values, this is often a good strategy for families where the parent is not expected to live much longer.

Where the parent has a longer life expectancy, however, there is a danger that the adverse Capital Gains Tax considerations will outweigh any Inheritance Tax savings. (As we saw in Chapter 12, the purchaser will not be exempt from Capital Gains Tax on a sale of the property!)

13.7 THE WIDOW'S LOAN SCHEME & THE FAMILY HOME

The method described in Section 4.6 works just as well for the family home as for any other assets. Probably better, in fact, as there is an asset on which to secure the loan and thus give it the necessary commercial substance.

13.8 LEAVE A HALF SHARE TO THE CHILDREN

You could simply leave your half share in the property to your children, who will then, after your death, own it jointly with your surviving spouse.

As long as the house is not worth in excess of twice the nil rate band, there will be no Inheritance Tax on it on your death.

This is fine as long as you are happy that your children, and, more particularly, their spouses or partners, will all get along OK with your spouse after you're gone.

Furthermore, the surviving spouse's remaining joint share in the property should give them a continuing right of occupation.

In practice though, this simple route often causes difficulty and families in this situation have been known to come to blows (both metaphorically and physically).

The other joint owners can sometimes even force a sale of the former family home against the wishes of the surviving spouse.

However, there is a way around these practical problems, as follows:

i) After inheriting a half share in the property, the children set up a trust, with their surviving parent as both trustee and beneficiary, and transfer their share into it.

ii) The provisions of the trust are that the property reverts to the children, as settlors, on the death of the surviving parent.

As explained in Section 9.7, for trusts set up before 22nd March 2006, this method worked very well, since, when property reverted to the settlor of an 'old-style' interest in possession trust, the transfer was exempt from Inheritance Tax.

Sadly, any new trusts of this kind after 22nd March 2006 will be treated as relevant property trusts (see Chapter 9) and there will be a risk of anniversary and exit charges arising.

Nevertheless, these charges may well be substantially less than the amount saved by keeping half of the property out of the surviving spouse's estate.

Meanwhile, the more recently deceased parent will have also left the other half share in the property, which they owned absolutely, to the children and their nil rate band will still be available to eliminate, or at least substantially reduce, any Inheritance Tax.

13.9   THE 'FULL CONSIDERATION' METHOD

The 'Gifts with Reservation' rules can be bypassed if, after giving the property to your children, you then pay them a full commercial rent for continuing to live in the property.

Payment of the rent would also help to further reduce your estate for Inheritance Tax purposes.

The major drawback to this method is the fact that your children would have to account for Income Tax on the rent which you are paying to them.

This is likely to render this method impractical in reality in some cases.

13.10 CO-OWNERSHIP

This method is very popular with widows and widowers (or other single parents) who have mature single adult children.

Quite simply, you just put the property into joint ownership with one or more of your children and then live together with them in the house.

The transfer of one or more shares in the house is a Potentially Exempt Transfer as long as the child or children are living there.

It is the children's presence in the house that prevents the transfer from being a 'Gift with Reservation'.

However, if one or more of the donee children should subsequently move out of the property whilst the parent themselves is still in occupation, the only way to prevent the 'Gift with Reservation' rules from destroying this Inheritance Tax planning strategy would be for the parent to then pay a market rent for their use of the appropriate share of the property.

It is also important that each party bears their own share of the household running costs. If any child were to pay the full household running costs, or even just part of the parent's share, after the transfer, then a 'Gift with Reservation' would have taken place and the Inheritance Tax planning will be undone.

13.11 SHEARING

The Inheritance Tax on the house can be reduced by dividing up the legal interests in the property in such a way that there is no 'Gift with Reservation'.

Due to anti-avoidance rules, to use this method, the transferor must have owned the property for at least seven years.

If the property is held jointly by a couple, each of them must have owned their own share for at least seven years.

This method is generally only effective when there is no intention of selling the property, i.e. it is to be retained in the family, even after the original owner's death.

This is how it works:

i) Create a long-term lease over the property which becomes effective some years from now (say in 15 or 20 years' time).
ii) Grant that lease to an interest in possession trust with your children as the beneficiaries and you (and your spouse or partner, if applicable) as trustee.

The duration of the lease needs to be long enough to ensure that you will never benefit from your freehold reversion after its expiry. The strategy works best with a very lengthy lease, say for 999 years.

The start date for the lease needs to be chosen on the basis of the donor's life expectancy, but cannot be more than 21 years after its execution.

As the clock runs down towards the time when the lease comes into effect, the value of your freehold interest in the property reduces.

Hopefully, if you time it right, at the time of your death, your interest in the house will have minimal value and will easily be covered by the nil rate band.

What If You Live Too Long?

If you, or your spouse or partner, are fortunate enough to survive long enough to still be around when the lease comes into effect then, in order to avoid the 'Gifts with Reservation' rules, you could start paying a commercial rent to your children (but see Section 13.9 above re Income Tax).

Alternatively, by that stage, you may well be happy to move into something smaller!

Wealth Warnings

Revenue & Customs' Capital Taxes Office claim that this scheme no longer works for leases granted after 8th March 1999.

Many prominent tax advisers do not agree with this view but, as yet, the matter has not been tested in the Courts.

Furthermore, for a new interest in possession trust created on or after 22nd March 2006, anniversary and exit charges will apply to the value of the lease within the trust.

This method may still be beneficial in some circumstances, however.

Alternatives to avoid these charges might include using a bare trust or granting the lease directly to the children, or even to company, but the position on these is not yet certain.

13.12 THE THREE-WAY SPLIT

Several of the above methods are designed to avoid Inheritance Tax on a house worth up to twice the amount of the nil rate band.

This scheme, however, may possibly exempt a house worth up to three times the amount of the nil rate band (i.e. £855,000 at current rates).

To follow this method we need to make an assumption about which spouse will die first. If we get this wrong, the survivor will have to think again (but should not get an immediate Inheritance Tax bill).

For the sake of illustration, let's assume that the husband will probably die first (statistics would support us on this).

First, if the house is in England or Wales, we put it into a tenancy in common.

Next, we divide up the ownership of the house so that two thirds of the ownership goes to the husband and one third to the wife.

On the husband's death he leaves half of his share (i.e. one third of the total) to a life interest trust in favour of his wife, with the remainder to the children. This should still qualify as an immediate post-death interest (see Section 9.8) and hence be counted within the wife's estate and also an exempt transfer on the husband's death.

The husband leaves the other half of his share (again one third of the total) to a discretionary trust, thus utilising his nil rate band. At some convenient date prior to the first ten-year anniversary, this trust can be wound up and the property share will be passed to the children. Alternatively, to protect the widow, it may be better to keep the trust going and pay some modest anniversary charges.

The wife does agree, however, to an early termination of her life interest and passes that one third share of the property to the children. This will be a potentially exempt transfer and will be exempt from Inheritance Tax as long as the wife survives another seven years.

Ultimately, when the widow dies herself, her nil rate band can be utilised against her remaining one third share of the property.

Chapter 14

Income Tax Charges on Pre-Owned Assets

14.1 MOVING THE GOALPOSTS

On 10th December 2003, the Chancellor of the Exchequer, Gordon Brown, announced proposals for a new Income Tax charge on many families who had previously attempted to plan for the future by making gifts of property or other assets.

Sadly, despite many representations to the contrary, particularly from the accountancy profession, this appalling piece of legislation has now come into force.

We are used to Revenue & Customs moving the goalposts but, this time, they've taken the ball home and come back with an entirely different game.

Nevertheless, we now have to accept that, from 6th April 2005, an Income Tax charge, known as the 'Pre-Owned Asset Charge', will, in many circumstances, be levied on the former owner of any asset who continues to benefit from that asset.

In many cases, the charge will also extend to a donor who benefits from the use of assets purchased with funds which they had previously gifted.

Typically, in the case of 'real' property, (i.e. land and buildings), the 'benefit' arises by reason of the fact that the donor continues to live in the property.

The property or other assets which are subject to the charge are known as 'pre-owned assets' and, broadly, the new charge taxes the 'annual value' of these assets as a benefit-in-kind on the former owner still enjoying their use, or otherwise benefiting from them.

For a property, the annual value on which the charge is based is the property's open-market rental value.

For most other assets to which the charge applies, the charge is based on a fixed percentage of their capital value. This percentage, in turn, is based on current interest rates and has initially been set at 5%.

The values to be used in these calculations are those prevailing at the beginning of the first tax year to which the charge applies or, if later, the date on which the asset first falls within these provisions. Hence, in most cases, the relevant valuation date will be 6th April 2005.

For property and most other types of tangible assets, the initial value derived as above can be used for a total of five tax years before the asset must be revalued.

Any amounts that the former owner is paying for the use of the asset may be deducted from the annual value in arriving at the taxable benefit. These payments must be made under a legal obligation, however, so, in the case of property, a formal lease will be required.

The pre-owned assets charge is designed to hit back at a number of Inheritance Tax planning schemes, but will also catch many unintended and innocent victims.

14.2 EXEMPTIONS

Thankfully, however, there are a few exemptions from this new charge, which, broadly speaking, will not apply where:

i)   The asset was gifted before 18th March 1986.

ii)   The asset was transferred to the donor's spouse, or to a former spouse under the terms of a court order.

iii) The asset was transferred to a trust for the benefit of the donor's spouse, or to a trust for the benefit of a former spouse under the terms of a court order. This exemption will cease to apply if the transferee spouse or former spouse's interest in possession (see Chapter 9) has come to an end other than on their death.

iv) The asset was transferred for the purposes of 'maintenance of family' (as explained in Sections 6.6 and 6.7).

v) There was an outright gift of the asset to an individual, which was wholly covered by the annual exemption or the small gifts exemption.

vi) The asset was acquired with funds derived from an earlier gift by the taxpayer which itself would have fallen within one or more of items (i) to (v) above.

vii) The asset is, in fact, still in your estate for Inheritance Tax purposes, or is treated as such due to the Gifts with Reservation Rules (hence, you generally shouldn't get caught for both taxes on the same asset).

viii) The asset was sold on normal, commercial, arm's length terms (even if to a connected party). Note that this exclusion can only apply to a sale of the taxpayer's entire interest in the asset, and does not cover a sale of part of his or her interest in an asset. (But see (ix) and (x) below.)

ix) A part interest in an asset is also exempted if it was sold to an unconnected party on normal, commercial, arm's length terms.

x) A part interest in an asset which was sold to a connected party on normal, commercial, arm's length terms may be exempted if it was sold either:
   a. Before 7th March 2005, or
   b. For a consideration not in the form of money or other assets readily convertible into money.

xi) The donor of the asset had themselves inherited it and their ownership had ceased as a result of a Deed of Variation affecting that inheritance (see Section 15.10).

xii) The donor's continued enjoyment of the asset has arisen only as a result of an unforeseen change in circumstances which has left them unable to care for themselves.

xiii) The donor's enjoyment of the asset is minor and incidental, such as social visits to the current occupier.

xiv) The donor's total annual taxable benefits under the pre-owned asset rules, ***before*** deducting any contributions paid by the donor, do not exceed £5,000. Note that this is an 'all or nothing' exemption and, if total taxable benefits reach £5,001, then the ***whole*** of this sum (less any donor contributions) is taxed!

xv) The asset was acquired with funds derived from an outright gift of money (sterling or foreign) made seven years or more before the donor first enjoyed any benefit from the asset.

xvi) The original gift of the asset was exempt for Inheritance Tax purposes under one of the exemptions in Section 4.8.

xvii) The donor has retained a suitable interest in the gifted asset, such as in the case of a parent who has given a joint share in a property to an adult child who lives with them in that property. This exemption would not apply, however, where the parent gave their adult child cash or another asset with which the child funded their share of a joint purchase.

xviii) The donor is non-UK resident.

Revenue & Customs has also confirmed that the charge should not apply in most cases where a taxpayer has funded life policies held on trust (see Section 11.9).

The charge is also excluded where the taxpayer has merely acted as a guarantor in respect of a loan made to another person to enable them to acquire the relevant asset.

Connected Persons

For the purposes of the pre-owned assets charge, the normal list of persons regarded as 'connected' for tax purposes (see Appendix C) is further extended to also include aunts, uncles, nieces and nephews, as well as companies under their control and trusts of which they are a beneficiary.

14.3   OPTING OUT

There is a 'Get Out Of Jail - But Not Free' card in the shape of an option to elect out of the pre-owned assets Income Tax charge, but only by allowing the property to be included back in the donor's estate for Inheritance Tax purposes.

The asset is then effectively treated as remaining in the donor's estate for as long as they continue to enjoy a benefit from it. Hence, in the case of a property, if the donor moves out and manages to survive for seven years, they will have managed to avoid both the Income Tax charge and the Inheritance Tax on the relevant asset.

The catch? The average life expectancy of a person going into residential care is approximately two years.

The election to opt out of the pre-owned asset charge must be made by the 31st January following the tax year in which the charge would otherwise have first arisen.

Most such elections will therefore need to be made by 31st January 2007!

14.4   IMPLICATIONS FOR PLANNING WITH THE FAMILY HOME

Several of the planning techniques outlined in the previous chapter involve the taxpayer or their surviving spouse having continued enjoyment of their family home.

Hence, at this stage, it is necessary for us to assess the potential impact of the new pre-owned assets charge on these planning techniques:

'Move Out and Then Give It Away' (13.2)

No charges should arise as long as the donor never moves back into the property, or only does so due to an unforeseen change in circumstances which has left them unable to care for themselves.

Care must also be taken that the donor never benefits from any other asset purchased with the proceeds of a subsequent sale of the original property.

'Sell Up and Give Away The Proceeds' (13.3),
'Re-Mortgage and Give Away The Proceeds' (13.4) and
'Re-Mortgage and Buy An Annuity' (13.5)

There should be no problems with any of these techniques as long as the donor does not benefit from the use of any asset purchased with the sale proceeds within a period of seven years after making their cash gifts.

Some concern has arisen, however, regarding a variation of the technique discussed in Section 13.5, under which many retired people have given their property to a financial institution in exchange for an annuity (often known as 'Equity Release Schemes').

At first, it appeared that these people would become innocent victims of the new pre-owned asset charge. I say 'innocent' because, clearly, such people were merely providing for their own financial needs in retirement and not even trying to avoid any Inheritance Tax.

Thankfully, however, on 7th March 2005, Paymaster General Dawn Primarolo confirmed that the pre-owned asset charge would not apply to any property simply because all or part of it is the subject of a commercial equity release scheme. (A charge might still apply, however, if some other, non-commercial, factor is involved in respect of the property.)

'Sale At Market Value' (13.6) and
'Widow's Loan Scheme' (when applied to the family home, 13.7)

No pre-owned asset charge can arise under these techniques.

'Leave A Half Share To The Children' (13.8)

There are two danger areas to be aware of here.

Firstly, if the surviving spouse had originally given a half share in the property to their deceased spouse, or had given them the funds with which to purchase that half share, and had done so before they were married or in a registered civil partnership, then the pre-owned asset charge will arise.

Secondly, where children, or other beneficiaries under the deceased's Will, have placed their share of the property into a life interest trust for the benefit of the deceased's spouse, they must be careful not to have any use or enjoyment of the property during the life interest of the surviving spouse. If the children, or other beneficiaries under the deceased's Will, were to use the property whilst the life interest trust continued, they would face a pre-owned asset charge. Minor and incidental use of the property, such as limited social visits, is, however, permitted.

Otherwise, apart from these two danger areas, the new charge should not apply where this technique is used.

The 'Full Consideration' Method (13.9)

This method should be unaffected by the new charge, owing to the fact that the donor of the property is making full payment for their continued use of it.

It is **essential**, however, that the donor's rental payments are made under a legal obligation to do so, i.e. a lease, and are reviewed every five years, in line with the pre-owned assets revaluation rules.

'Co-Ownership' (13.10)

Revenue & Customs have specifically confirmed that this method will not be caught under the new charge.

'Shearing' (13.11)

Revenue & Customs seem to think that this method no longer works for Inheritance Tax purposes, as they believe that a 'Gift with Reservation' occurs.

If they're right then no charge under the pre-owned asset rules can apply.

How then, could they attempt to enforce such a charge?

If, however, we believe the many prominent tax advisers who state that this scheme does still work, then we must also interpret the new legislation as meaning that a pre-owned asset charge **does** arise.

Until we get a ruling on this scheme from the Courts, therefore, this will continue to present something of a dilemma!

What is beyond doubt is that anyone who undertook this type of scheme before 9th March 1999 will be subject to the pre-owned asset charge on the value of the lease granted to their trust or their beneficiaries.

'The Three-Way Split' (13.12)

As with 'Leave a Half Share to the Children', there is a risk of a pre-owned asset charge if the survivor had funded the purchase of the property prior to marriage. Otherwise, the scheme would appear to avoid the pre-owned assets charge.

14.5   TAX CHARGES AND DOMICILE

For UK resident and domiciled taxpayers (see Chapter 16), the charge applies to any relevant assets worldwide, except as noted below. This extends to those with deemed UK domicile for Inheritance Tax purposes (see Section 2.2).

For those who did not have a UK 'Domicile of Origin' (see Chapter 16), but who have subsequently acquired actual or deemed UK domicile, the charge will not apply to any non-UK assets that they transferred into a trust before acquiring UK domicile or deemed UK domicile.

For taxpayers who are UK resident, but non-UK domiciled and also not deemed UK domiciled, the pre-owned asset charge can apply only to any relevant assets situated in the UK.

Chapter 15

The Inheritance Tax Planning Timetable

15.1 IT'S NEVER TOO EARLY TO START

Most tax advisers will tell you that it's never too early to start Inheritance Tax planning.

Nevertheless, when you're struggling to pay a massive mortgage and to make some headway at the beginning of your working career, it will appear that there's not much point in thinking about Inheritance Tax.

However, as we saw in Section 10.4, the earlier you start, the more effective your planning will be, and if you are lucky enough to have the wealth to follow the kind of planning in that section, long term planning will help to pass on more family wealth to the next generation, or even the one after that.

Even if you have little wealth, your first step should be to ensure that any life policies are written into trust.

15.2 MARRIAGE

First of all, marriage is a good time to remind the family to do their Inheritance Tax planning by making the exempt gifts set out in Section 6.5.

Next, remember to make a new Will. An existing Will is rendered void on marriage or civil partnership unless it was actually made in contemplation of your union.

Once you are married, you need to think about how to make sure you each use your nil rate band.

15.3 BECOMING A PARENT

This is the one which focuses the mind and gets most people thinking about Inheritance Tax planning.

It's time to step up the ante a little and begin to think about tax efficient trust structures for your children, perhaps some bare trusts will come in handy?

It's time to re-write your Will again as well, especially to incorporate provision for a 'trust for a bereaved minor'.

15.4 ADULT CHILDREN

You can now start giving assets directly to the children without the need for any trust structures. Making use of the annual exemption may make sense, although most of us seem to have little choice anyway!

Normal expenditure out of income can be established to pass on substantial sums to the children and when they marry, you can use the exemptions in Section 6.5.

15.5 YOUR FIRST GRANDCHILD

Time to start looking at trust structures again and you will probably also want to re-write your Will again.

Maybe you should start to think about 'skipping a generation'. What's the point of leaving the money to the children if they're already well established? It might be better left to the grandchildren, so that Inheritance Tax doesn't come up again for another two generations.

Bare trusts for grandchildren are really useful and avoid the 'Gift with Reservation' problems which you tend to get with your own minor children.

15.6 LIFE EXPECTANCY OVER SEVEN YEARS

(Per actuarial tables, this is men aged under 80 and women under 83)

There's still time to make potentially exempt transfers which should hopefully have time to become fully exempt.

Terminating the 'reservation' on a 'Gift with Reservation' will give it time to become exempt also.

Remember, as long as you survive at least three years, some savings will be made.

15.7 LIFE EXPECTANCY THREE TO SEVEN YEARS

(Men aged 80 to 93 and women aged 83 to 94)

Transfers made now should at least still benefit from tapering (see Section 5.5), so some tax will be saved.

It's time to really start making the most of the annual exemption, the small gifts exemption and normal expenditure out of income.

A loan trust will really make sense at this point, and possibly also gifts of appreciating assets not qualifying for business property relief, as long as Capital Gains Tax can be avoided (but refer back to Chapter 12 for a more thorough analysis).

15.8 LIFE EXPECTANCY TWO TO THREE YEARS

(Men aged 93 to 99 and women aged 94 to 100)

Now's the time to think seriously about those AIM shares, but never forgetting 'Dodgy Dave' (see Section 11.2).

Seriously though, anything which gets your money into qualifying business property (see Chapter 7) may still enable you to avoid Inheritance Tax if you can survive two years.

Loan trusts and reversionary interest trusts may still save you money even now, as well as other transfers of appreciating property (but watch the Capital Gains Tax situation).

15.9 DEATHBED PLANNING

So, if you've really left it far too late, what can still be done?

Some of this may seem a little flippant and I have no wish to cause any offence to anyone. Tax planning may be the farthest thing from your mind at this point and who could really blame you.

Nevertheless, here are some of the things you could think about if time is running out:

Deathbed Marriage

The biggest deathbed planning point, if you're still single at this stage, is to marry your partner. No point trying to hang on to your freedom now, just get on with it!

Entering a 'deathbed' registered civil partnership will also produce the same effect.

Ideally, you do need a partner for this, but, if you really hate the Government and have no-one else to leave your money to, just marry anyone! (Although leaving it all to your favourite charity would probably make more sense.)

Last Gasp Gifts

If you haven't used up your annual exemption (see Section 6.2) for this, or the previous, tax year, get gifting.

If you've made no previous gifts, one simple £6,000 payment to one of your nearest and dearest will save your family £2,400.

For the rest of your family and friends, there's the Small Gifts Exemption (see Section 6.3). Every person you can find to give £250 to will save your estate £100 in Inheritance Tax. Perhaps you have something better to do with your last days, but, just think, every cheque you write could be worth £100 to your estate!

Remember, however, as explained in Section 5.7, that these gifts will not be effective unless the cheques clear through the transferee's bank account before you pass away.

What About The House?

Your family will be able to achieve a great deal by using a Deed of Variation (see Section 15.10). However, if your house is held in a joint tenancy, it will pass by survivorship and there will be nothing they can do.

Change the title to a tenancy in common and your family can do the rest of the planning later.

Remember Your Normal Gifts

The exemption for normal expenditure out of income (see Section 6.8) applies to lifetime gifts only.

To get that final year's exemption you need to make sure you've made that expenditure before you go.

Spend!

"There are no pockets in shrouds" they say, so why not spend it before Gordon Brown gets hold of it.

"How will this help my family?" you may ask, but think about this:

Example

Ian knows he has only a few months to live and wants to give his friend Chas a last gift.

What Chas would really like is a new car and the model he has his eye on, a 'Rhythm Stick Blockhead', costs £25,000 new.

Ian therefore buys a 'Rhythm Stick Blockhead' but doesn't give it to Chas straight away. Instead, Ian leaves the car to Chas in his Will.

When Ian dies a few months later, the car, now second-hand, is worth only £18,000 and this is the value to be used for Inheritance Tax purposes.

If Ian had simply given the car to Chas brand new, a sum of £25,000 would have been included in his estate. Hence, by leaving the car in his Will instead, Ian has saved up to £2,800 in Inheritance Tax.

Contractual Obligations

The liabilities under any contractual obligations existing at the date of your death will be deductible from your estate.

Hence, if your beneficiaries would like something done to any asset which is about to pass to them under the terms of your Will, why not contract for the work to be done at your expense?

Review Your Will

Whilst you're still of sound mind, there is still time to change your Will.

Any measures to use the nil rate band (see Section 4.4) should be top of the list.

Your beneficiaries can always do a Deed of Variation within the next two years as long as all affected parties agree. What you might need to consider at this stage, however, is whether there are any beneficiaries in your current Will who are likely to stand in the way of any Inheritance Tax saving measures by refusing to agree to a Deed of Variation.

The easiest way to save Inheritance Tax at this stage is, of course, to change your Will to leave some or all of your estate to charity (but not a foreign charity!), although your existing beneficiaries may not be entirely happy about this. Still, it's your decision (mostly – see Section 11.8).

Go Home Or Stay Away

In Chapter 16, we will look in detail at the issues of either retaining a foreign 'Domicile of Origin' or obtaining a foreign 'Domicile of Choice'.

In borderline cases, the final outcome regarding your domicile will be heavily influenced by your final actions. To keep a foreign Domicile of Origin, it may be wise to go home to die.

Conversely, to maintain a foreign 'Domicile of Choice' it will be best if you remain in your adopted country.

Buying a grave plot and arranging your funeral in your new adopted country will also be helpful to your cause.

Maximise Your Business Property

Whilst, as explained in Section 7.11, the business property itself needs to have been held for at least two years in order to qualify for business property relief, you can enhance the value of existing business property at any time.

This might, for example, include:

- Paying business debts from private resources
- Transferring assets into a qualifying private company (see Section 7.16 for more details)

Transferring assets to a company may, however, have Capital Gains Tax consequences and these must be borne in mind.

Deathbed Capital Gains Tax Planning

What you (probably) should **not** do at this stage is to make any disposals which give rise to Capital Gains Tax liabilities.

If you sell assets before you die, your estate will be liable for the Capital Gains Tax arising based on your original base costs for those assets. Subject to this liability, however, the proceeds of the sale will remain in your estate and will still be subject to Inheritance Tax.

If you hang on to those assets, the Inheritance Tax may be a little greater (as there is no Capital Gains Tax liability to deduct) but, as we saw in Chapter 12, your Personal Representatives or your beneficiaries will be able to sell them later with little or no Capital Gains Tax liability.

Conversely, therefore, the best deathbed planning for Capital Gains Tax purposes may be to accumulate more assets!

15.10 DEEDS OF VARIATION

Perhaps the 'last resort' in Inheritance Tax planning is the Deed of Variation.

Deeds of Variation are an essential planning tool where a family finds that the terms of the deceased's Will (or intestacy) have an undesired effect for Inheritance Tax purposes.

Where all affected beneficiaries are in agreement, it is possible to vary the Will in order to create a better Inheritance Tax result (e.g. to utilise the deceased's nil rate band).

As the Deed of Variation is a legally binding document, it is essential to consult a lawyer when completing it.

Conditions

i) The required variations must be recorded in writing within two years of the death (this is the Deed).

ii) All those persons affected by the variations to the Will or intestacy, and any other persons who benefit from the variations, should sign the Deed.

iii) If the variation affects the amount of Inheritance Tax payable as a result of the deceased's death, an election must be made in writing to Revenue & Customs within six months after the date of the Deed by the persons in (ii) above. If the variation results in an increase in the

Inheritance Tax becoming payable, the deceased's Personal Representatives must also sign the election.

iv) The variation must not be made for any consideration in money or money's worth, except in the case of other compensatory variations to the deceased's Will or intestacy.

Variations made by such a Deed are treated for Inheritance Tax purposes as if they had been made by the deceased.

This means that a surviving spouse who becomes a party to a Deed of Variation and, as a result, gives up a right to a part of their inheritance, is not themselves regarded as having made any transfer of value (neither chargeable nor otherwise).

Chapter 16

Domicile

16.1 WHAT IS DOMICILE?

In essence, your 'Domicile' is the country which you consider to be your permanent home.

This does not necessarily equate to your country of birth, nor to the country in which you happen to be living at present.

Furthermore, 'Domicile' should not be confused with residence, which is a far more transitory concept (but see Section 2.2 regarding deemed domicile).

At this point, it is worth noting that, technically speaking, you cannot actually have 'UK Domicile' but will, instead, have your domicile in England and Wales, Scotland or Northern Ireland.

This can be very important when it comes to intestacy or the question of 'legal rights', as we saw in Sections 11.7 and 11.8.

For Inheritance Tax itself, however, it is safe to simply refer to 'UK Domicile'.

It is also worth noting that the Channel Islands and the Isle of Man are not part of the UK for tax purposes, including Inheritance Tax and Domicile.

16.2 DOMICILE OF ORIGIN

At birth, each person acquires the 'Domicile' of the person on whom they are legally dependent at that time. That person will, in most cases, be their father, but it is their mother, if either:

i) Their father is dead at the time of their birth, or
ii) Their parents are both alive, but living apart, and they have a home with their mother, but do not have a home with their father.

The domicile which you acquire at birth is known as your 'Domicile of Origin'.

Throughout your minority, you continue to have the same Domicile as the person on whom you are legally dependent.

You only become capable of having your own independent domicile when you reach whichever of the following ages is applicable, or marry under that age. The applicable ages are:

    i)   In England, Wales and Northern Ireland, the age of 16.
    ii) In Scotland, for a boy, the age of 14.
    iii) In Scotland, for a girl, the age of 12.

Example

Farouk was born in Zanzibar in 1946. He lived with both of his unmarried parents at that time. His father was domiciled in India and his mother was domiciled in Tanzania. Farouk therefore acquired Indian domicile at birth and this was his Domicile of Origin.

In 1960, Farouk's mother left his father, taking Farouk with her, and moved to England. She did not intend to make the UK her permanent home, however, and intended to return to Tanzania when circumstances permitted.

At this point, Farouk therefore acquired Tanzanian domicile (i.e. his mother's). This became his new Domicile of Origin. Your Domicile of Origin can only change during your minority; once you have become capable of having your own independent domicile (see above), it cannot be changed.

Assuming this position continued until his 16th birthday, Farouk would then acquire a final Domicile of Origin of Tanzania.

16.3   DOMICILE OF CHOICE

In most cases, a person's Domicile of Origin remains their Domicile for the rest of their life.

This Domicile can only be changed, to a 'Domicile of Choice', through permanent emigration (and, in this case, I <u>mean</u> permanent).

Acquiring a new domicile for tax purposes, as a 'Domicile of Choice', can be very difficult to prove. This is both good news and bad news since it cuts both ways and Revenue & Customs have had just as much difficulty proving that a taxpayer has acquired the UK as his Domicile of Choice as taxpayers have had in proving that they have acquired a Domicile somewhere else.

To acquire a new Domicile, as a Domicile of Choice, it is necessary to not only demonstrate an intention to adopt the new country as your permanent home, but also to follow this up by action and subsequent conduct.

If the taxpayer abandons their Domicile of Choice, their Domicile automatically reverts to their Domicile of Origin.

Example

Brian is UK Domiciled. However, in 2006, he decides to emigrate permanently to Australia and thus become Australian Domiciled.

He declares this intention on form P85, which he lodges with the UK Revenue & Customs shortly before he departs for Sydney.

In 2007, Brian gets a terrific offer to work in California, so he leaves Australia to adopt the USA as his new permanent home.

Brian's Domicile has now reverted to the UK!

Wealth Warning

If you intend to emigrate to avoid UK Inheritance Tax, make sure you pick the right country first time!

Although Brian might eventually be able to establish US Domicile, this will now be very difficult for him because he has established a 'track record' of abandoning his so-called 'permanent home'.

How now could he possibly prove that he has no intention of ever returning to the UK?

Wealth Warning Part 2

The other point to note about emigrating to avoid Inheritance Tax is that you will also be _deemed_ to be UK Domiciled at the time of your death if you were actually still UK Domiciled under general principles at any time in the preceding three years.

As explained in Section 2.2, this may be affected by one of the Double Tax Treaties referred to in Appendix B.

Emigrating for this purpose must therefore be done early and carefully.

16.4   A GUIDE TO EMIGRATION

There is no set procedure for establishing a Domicile of Choice through permanent emigration.

Like many things in the tax world, each individual case will be examined on its own particular merits.

Here, however, are a few practical tips to follow:

- Declare your intentions to Revenue & Customs on form P85 before leaving the UK (see Section 16.7).

- Buy a home in your new country.

- Take your family with you.

- Take whatever steps you can to establish citizenship, nationality, etc, in your new country.

- Take up employment in your new country (or, alternatively, establish your own business there).

- Get on the electoral roll in your new country.

- Buy a grave plot in your new country (this is given a great deal of importance by the tax authorities when looking at Domicile).

- Try to visit the UK as little as possible.

- Sell as many UK assets as you can.

- Resign membership of any clubs, associations, etc, in the UK.

- Write a Will in your new country.

- DO NOT MOVE ON AGAIN TO ANOTHER COUNTRY!

16.5   RETAINING A DOMICILE OF ORIGIN

If you are lucky enough to have a non-UK Domicile of Origin it is far, far, easier to retain this as your Domicile than it is to acquire a Domicile of Choice.

As stated above, it is very difficult for Revenue & Customs to prove that an individual has acquired a new Domicile of Choice.

This is especially true if the individual themselves states that it is their intention to return to their country of origin one day.

In <u>this</u> case, an 'intention' does not have to be backed up by action.

Example

Thais was born in Brazil, of Brazilian parents. She has, however, lived in the UK for over 40 years, having moved here in her early twenties. Despite this, she has always stated that she intends to return 'home' before she dies.

Thais remains Domiciled in Brazil.

However, as explained above, Thais would be deemed to be UK Domiciled for Inheritance Tax purposes, as she has been resident here for at least 17 of the last 20 years.

Tax Tip

If you have a foreign Domicile of Origin, it is worth retaining this for UK tax purposes as, even if you acquire deemed domicile for Inheritance Tax purposes, your foreign domicile will still provide opportunities to defer or avoid Income Tax and Capital Gains Tax.

To ensure that you don't end up with deemed UK Domicile for Inheritance Tax purposes, you should try to spend four years out of every twenty abroad (or one in five, if you prefer). This does not have to be in the same country as your Domicile of Origin.

You should also complete a form DOM 1, declaring yourself to be non-Domiciled, and submit it to the Financial Intermediaries and Claims Office (see Section 16.7 below).

When completing your Tax Return, you should tick the boxes in Question 9 on page 2 and complete pages NR1 and NR2 as appropriate. Technically, you are only supposed to do this if you actually have some unremitted foreign income or gains. However, it is sensible to establish your non-domiciled position as much as possible.

Finally, it may be worth buying a grave plot in the country which is your Domicile of Origin. This is accepted as a very strong indication of your intention to return to that country at some future date.

16.6 DOMICILE AND MARRIAGE

Marriage does not affect a man's Domicile and it never has.

For women married on or after 1st January 1974, marriage again has no effect on their Domicile.

For women married before 1st January 1974, the position is as follows:

- **Non-US Nationals:**
  You adopt your husband's Domicile at the date of marriage. If this changed at any time before 1st January 1974, and you were still married and not legally separated at that time, then yours will have changed with his. You will continue to have the same Domicile as you thus had on 1st January 1974 unless you have subsequently adopted a new Domicile of Choice, or re-adopted your Domicile of Origin in the same way as anyone else would adopt a Domicile of Choice.

- **US Nationals:**
  Your Domicile is unaffected by your marriage.

16.7   ADMINISTRATION

Where relevant, forms P85 or DOM 1 should be sent to:

Revenue & Customs
Financial Intermediaries and Claims Office*
St John's House
Merton Road
Bootle
Merseyside
England
L69 9BB

(Tel: +44 151 472 6196)

* Also known as 'FICO'

Inheritance Tax Exemptions 2006/2007

Nil Rate Band:	£285,000
Transfers to Non-Domiciled Spouse:	£55,000
Annual Exemption:	£3,000*
Small Gifts Exemption:	£250
Gifts in consideration of marriage:	
Parents:	£5,000
Grandparents, etc:	£2,500
To Each other:	£2,500
Other Donors:	£1,000

*NB: 2005/2006 annual exemption of £3,000 may be added if not previously utilised and 2006/2007 annual exemption is exhausted.

Appendix B

Double Tax Treaties

Countries with which the UK has Double Tax Treaties covering Inheritance Tax (and its overseas equivalents).

- France
- Irish Republic
- India
- Italy
- Netherlands
- Pakistan
- South Africa
- Sweden
- Switzerland
- USA

Appendix C

Connected Persons

Connected persons include the following:

Generally

- Husband or wife (but note that such transfers are usually exempt)
- Civil Partner (from 5th December 2005, again such transfers will usually be exempt)
- Mother, father or remoter ancestor
- Son, daughter or remoter descendant
- Brother or sister
- Mother-in-law, father-in-law, son-in-law, daughter-in-law, brother-in-law or sister-in-law
- Mother, father, son, daughter, brother or sister of your civil partner (from 5th December 2005)
- Business partners
- Companies under the control of the other party to the transaction or of any of his/her relatives as above
- Trustees of a trust where the other party to the transaction, or any of his/her relatives as above, is a beneficiary

Additionally, for the purposes of the pre-owned asset charge only (see Chapter 14)

- Aunts and Uncles
- Nephews and Nieces
- Companies under the control of any of these relatives
- Trustees of a trust where any of these relatives are a beneficiary

Example Documentation

<u>1. Memorandum recording a gift (Inheritance Tax liability remains with transferor in the first instance*)</u>

MEMORANDUM OF GIFT FROM

Roger Meadows of 3 Taylor Street, Penzance

TO

Ian Deacon of 4 Queen Street, Belfast

MEMORANDUM that on 15th May 2006 Roger Meadows transferred by way of gift to Ian Deacon the sum of one million pounds (£1,000,000).

Dated: 20th May 2006

Signed by Roger Meadows:

Signed by Ian Deacon:

* - Note: Any Inheritance Tax arising at the time of the transfer will be the transferor's liability. In practice, however, most transfers to other individuals will be potentially exempt transfers, meaning that no Inheritance Tax actually arises at that stage. Any further Inheritance Tax arising in the event of the transferor's death within the next seven years will usually be the transferee's liability. If this is not desired, a memorandum along the lines of item 3 below will be appropriate.

2. Memorandum recording transferee's liability for Inheritance Tax on a lifetime transfer

MEMORANDUM OF GIFT FROM

James Stewart of 15 Castle Street, Stirling

TO

Mary Stewart of 42 Palace Road, Linlithgow

MEMORANDUM that on 16th May 2006 James Stewart transferred by way of gift to Mary Stewart (subject to the payment of any Inheritance Tax) the assets listed in the schedule below to the intent that they have become and are the absolute property of Mary Stewart and IN CONSIDERATION of such transfer Mary Stewart undertook to pay any Inheritance Tax in respect of such gift assessed upon James Stewart or his Personal Representatives and indemnifies James Stewart and his Personal Representatives accordingly.

SCHEDULE

- Property at 87 Flodden Avenue, Berwick upon Tweed
- Ten thousand Ordinary £1 Shares in Darnley plc
- The sum of five thousand pounds (£5,000) in cash

Dated: 21st May 2006

Signed by James Stewart:

Signed by Mary Stewart:

3. Memorandum recording a gift (all Inheritance Tax to be borne by the transferor)

MEMORANDUM OF GIFT FROM

Noddy Hill of 6 Slade Street, Wolverhampton

TO

David Holder of 9 Flame Avenue, Birmingham

MEMORANDUM that on 28th February 2007 Noddy Hill transferred by way of gift to David Holder the sum of two million pounds (£2,000,000). The said Noddy Hill hereby further undertakes that he or his Personal Representatives shall pay any Inheritance Tax assessed in respect of such gift out of the assets of his general estate and indemnifies David Holder accordingly.

Dated: 28th February 2007

Signed by Noddy Hill:

Signed by David Holder:

National Bodies

Subject to certain anti-avoidance provisions, gifts to any of the following bodies are exempt from Inheritance Tax:

- The National Gallery
- The British Museum
- The National Museum of Scotland
- The National Museum of Wales
- The Ulster Museum
- Other similar institutions approved for this purpose by HM Treasury
- Other Museums or Art Galleries in the UK which are maintained by a local authority or UK University
- Any library whose main function is to provide teaching and research facilities for a UK University
- The Historic Buildings and Monuments Commission for England
- The National Trust
- The National Trust for Scotland
- The National Art Collections Fund
- The Trustees of the National Heritage Memorial Fund
- The Friends of the National Libraries
- The Historic Churches Preservation Trust
- Nature Conservancy Council for England
- Scottish National Heritage
- Countryside Council for Wales
- Any Local Authority
- Any Government Department
- Any University (or University College) in the UK
- Certain Health Service Bodies

Need Affordable & Expert Tax Planning Help?

Try Our Unique Question & Answer Service

The purpose of this guide is to provide you with detailed guidance on how to pay less inheritance tax.

Ultimately, you may want to take further action or obtain guidance personal to your circumstances.

Taxcafe.co.uk has a unique online tax service that provides access to highly qualified tax professionals at an affordable rate.

No matter how complex your question, they will provide you with some help through this service. The cost is just £69.95.

To find out more go to **www.taxcafe.co.uk** and click the Tax Questions button.

Pay Less Tax!

... with help from Taxcafe's unique tax guides and software

All products available online at www.taxcafe.co.uk

- ➢ **How to Avoid Property Tax** – Essential reading for property investors who want to know all the tips and tricks to follow to pay less tax on their property profits.

- ➢ **Using a Property Company to Save Tax** - How to massively increase your profits by using a property company... plus all the traps to avoid.

- ➢ **How to Avoid Inheritance Tax** – A-Z of inheritance tax planning, with clear explanations and numerous examples. Covers simple and sophisticated tax planning.

- ➢ **Tax Planning for Couples** – How married and unmarried couples can save thousands in income tax, capital gains tax, inheritance tax and national insurance using a variety of powerful tax planning techniques.

- ➢ **Non Resident & Offshore Tax Planning** – How to exploit non-resident tax status to reduce your tax bill, plus advice on using offshore trusts and companies.

- ➢ **The World's Best Tax Havens** – How to cut your taxes to zero and safeguard your financial freedom.

- ➢ **How to Avoid Stamp Duty** – Little known but perfectly legal trade secrets to reduce your stamp duty bill when buying or selling property.

- ➢ **Grow Rich with a Property ISA** – Find out how to invest in property tax free with an ISA.

- ➤ **Using a Company to Save Tax** – Everything you need to know about the tax benefits of using a company to run your business.

- ➤ **Bonus vs Dividend** – Shows how shareholder/directors of companies can save thousands in tax by choosing the optimal mix of bonus and dividend.

- ➤ **How to Avoid Tax on Your Stock Market Profits** – How to pay less capital gains tax, income tax and inheritance tax on your stock market investments and dealings.

- ➤ **Selling a Sole Trader Business** – A potential minefield with numerous traps to avoid but significant tax-saving opportunities.

- ➤ **How to Claim Tax Credits** – Even families with higher incomes can make successful tax credit claims. This guide shows how much you can claim and how to go about it.

- ➤ **Property Capital Gains Tax Calculator** – Unique software that performs complex capital gains tax calculations in seconds.

Disclaimer

1. Please note that this Tax Guide is intended as general guidance only for individual readers and does NOT constitute accountancy, tax, investment or other professional advice. Neither Taxcafe UK Limited nor the author can accept any responsibility or liability for loss which may arise from reliance on information contained in this Tax Guide.

2. Please note that tax legislation, the law and practices by government and regulatory authorities (e.g. Revenue & Customs) are constantly changing and the information contained in this Tax Guide is only correct as at the date of publication. We therefore recommend that for accountancy, tax, investment or other professional advice, you consult a suitably qualified accountant, tax specialist, independent financial adviser, or other professional adviser. Please also note that your personal circumstances may vary from the general examples given in this Tax Guide and your professional adviser will be able to give specific advice based on your personal circumstances.

3. This Tax Guide covers UK taxation only and any references to 'tax' or 'taxation' in this Tax Guide, unless the contrary is expressly stated, refer to UK taxation only. Please note that references to the 'UK' do not include the Channel Islands or the Isle of Man. Foreign tax implications are beyond the scope of this Tax Guide.

4. Whilst in an effort to be helpful, this Tax Guide may refer to general guidance on matters other than UK taxation, Taxcafe UK Limited is not expert in these matters and does not accept any responsibility or liability for loss which may arise from reliance on such information contained in this Tax Guide.

5. Please note that Taxcafe UK Limited has relied wholly on the expertise of the author in the preparation of the content of this Tax Guide. The author is not an employee of Taxcafe UK Limited but has been selected by Taxcafe UK Limited using reasonable care and skill to write the content of this Tax Guide.

Printed in the United Kingdom
by Lightning Source UK Ltd.
116957UKS00001B/82-159